An
ATLANTIC TRILOGY

An

ATLANTIC TRILOGY

TALES OF SURVIVAL AND TRAGEDY

GORDON SNOW

AN ATLANTIC TRILOGY
TALES OF SURVIVAL AND TRAGEDY

iUniverse books may be ordered through booksellers or by contacting:

iUniverse
1663 Liberty Drive
Bloomington, IN 47403
www.iuniverse.com
1-800-Authors (1-800-288-4677)

My Island Fishing Home was originally self-published in 1997 in Ottawa, Canada. Copyright © Gordon Snow and Judy Finn ISBN 0–9681978–0– 9.

Survival of Salmo was originally published in 1992 by Carlton Press, Inc., New York, N.Y. Copyright © by Gordon Snow ISBN 0–8062–4349–X.

ISBN: 978-1-4917-8189-0 (sc)
ISBN: 978-1-4917-8190-6 (e)

Library of Congress Control Number: 2015918082

Print information available on the last page.

iUniverse rev. date: 11/05/2015

CONTENTS

Book Two
Survival of Salmo

Book Three
The Whales at Point au Gaul

PREFACE

Intriguing tales of survival and tragedy very often fascinate us by tweaking our curiosity and **My Island Fishing Home, Survival of Salmo** and **Whales of Point au Gaul** fit that category. Through the various approaches to the subject matter, you will appreciate the significance of all three in total context even though various setting are involved.

My Island Fishing Home describes the activities of a family fishing enterprise during the summer of 1922 based on the personal memoirs of Thomas as told to his daughter, Judy Finn. The harsh conditions, as outlined, may be difficult for many to comprehend, but heightens the realism of making a living from fishing during that particular period. I have added certain events to the story based on my own personal knowledge.

Survival of Salmo is of a different type because here I take on the persona of an Atlantic salmon called Salmo who was born in Long Harbour River in Fortune Bay, in the Province of Newfoundland and Labrador, Canada. Salmo tells the story of his whole life from initial birth in the river, his descent downstream, years at sea and eventual return to his birthplace for spawning. His story is a learning experience and is based on biological fact.

Whales at Point au Gaul is an actual, personal account of the tragic beaching of a large pod of pilot whales in 1979 that may have been the largest beaching of this species ever recorded. It describes the scene of the beaching and the efforts made to try and release the whales to open sea again. The enormity of the task and the unconquerable odds that occurred instills a sense of disbelief that such an event could happen.

Author

Book One

MY ISLAND
FISHING HOME

Gordon Snow and Judy Finn

This story is dedicated
To all those fishing families
Who carved a livelihood from the sea
Around the shores of Newfoundland and Labrador

INTRODUCTION

Harbour Grace Island is located in Conception Bay on the east coast of the Province of Newfoundland and Labrador, Canada. It was used as a summer fishing location by a number of fishermen and their families from the Town of Harbour Grace. The families moved to the Island in the late spring and returned again to their permanent homes in the fall.

Thomas Snow, father of Judy Finn, recalls a typical summer in the year 1922. He takes the reader through the various phases of life's experiences as a fourteen-year-old and his own involvement in the fishing operation. His life as a family member and the responsibilities he had to shoulder, even at a young age, are revealed through his personal accounts. The hardships encountered through the isolationism and crude existence tested the endurance of all family members, most especially his mother.

In these pages, Thomas's own thoughts will provide you with a sense of his deeper feelings about this fishing way of life. The strength of the family unit is explored to show how important it was to fishing success. Share in the joys and the tragedy during a typical summer of a teenager as part of a fishing family. Probe the inner thoughts of family members as they go about their daily tasks. Relive the life of a fourteen-year-old who leaves his school, friends, and comfortable surroundings to help his father ply the fishing trade as part of a family fishing enterprise.

Try to identify yourself with him as he seeks contentment, and sometimes finds it, among the rigours of Island life. Learn how religion, education, hard work, and close family ties all play a part in reaching relative success. Observe how this simple way of life can teach you to live in harmony with nature and all its elements.

Let Thomas take you back for a while and share his life and the lives of those around him. You will become enriched and sometimes amused by the events as they unfold.

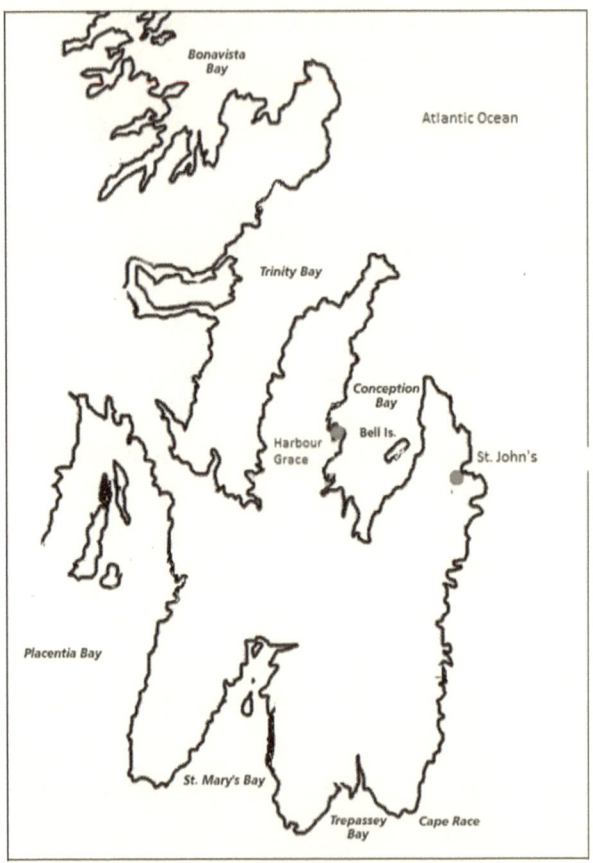

Location of Harbour Grace on the southeast portion of the island of Newfoundland.
(G. Snow)

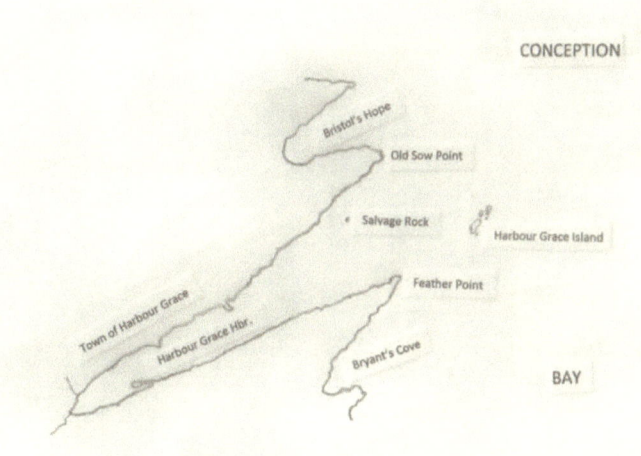

Harbour Grace showing proximity to Harbour Grace Island in Conception Bay.
(G. Snow)

Father, Thomas, and mother, Julia-Ann.

CHAPTER ONE

The Move

I stare at the sky from the shack door as I contemplate another adventurous fishing season on Fisherman's Island, one of a group of islands known locally as Harbour Grace Island. The Island is about three miles east of town, lying treeless and inconspicuously in Conception Bay, with the nearest mainland being Feather Point. Harbour Grace Island is actually six islands that include Fishermen's Island, where fishing operations take place. The remaining islands are Blackberry Island, Woody Island, two small islands called Pea Islands, and Lighthouse Island. The latter is the only other island with human habitation and is where the lighthouse keeper, Mr. Joe Morris, his wife, Winnie, and sons Fred and Frank live. He and his family are happy to have other families around in the summer and they often visit our island when weather is fine and he can leave his lighthouse responsibilities for short periods. We occasionally visit them, but only on a Sunday because that is the only day we don't fish. His sons began living in town during the academic year as soon as they became old enough to attend school.

Today has been exceptionally hectic in transporting our fishing gear, provisions, and other sundry supplies to our traditional summer residence. Father left no stone unturned to ensure we had accomplished our tasks successfully. This scene after all, is part of my family life and culture that has roots dating back more than 200 years. The essence of our existence here is planted in the veins of my ancestors and is now exemplified in my own mother and father. I wonder how much longer progeny like myself would continue to fulfil this annual ritual.

It makes practical sense to establish a summer residence on the Island for proximity to the fishing grounds. Had we operated from Harbour Grace, it would require a rowing trip of about two hours just to start fishing and only then if the weather was clement. We needed an area to set up fishing operations in which the whole family could participate, and thus Fisherman's Island became our fishing refuge along with eleven other families. Each summer it became the nucleus of our fishing operation in close association with the other families.

I learned in school that Harbour Grace was probably named by the French, who perceived a resemblance to the town of Havre de Grace in France at the mouth of the Seine. Jersey businessmen are believed to have done business here as early as 1560; they were prominent in other Newfoundland locations as well. John Guy established the first colony in Newfoundland for Britain in 1610 in nearby Cupids, and Harbour Grace capitalized on that event by encouraging businesses and individuals to settle here. Those early days were often interrupted by French attacks and looting along the east coast in the 1600s. Harbour Grace was the victim of such an attack in1696.

Harbour Grace also experienced the establishment of pirates under the capable hands of Captain Peter Easton, who located his headquarters in the east end of town around 1600. He and his fellow pirates controlled the area for a number of years. How exciting it must have been back then over 300 years ago. Now the only pirates we have relate to some of the merchants, or at least that is what I have heard them referred to on occasion.

From reading, I found out that in 1830 a jail and adjoining courthouse was constructed. For many, it indicated that the town needed the jail to contend with criminal activity. However, citizen-pride would rather believe a jail was a necessary part of growth and settlement. It was during this time that a flourishing seal industry and cod fishery led to the location of many business houses, and the town ranked second only to St. John's in trade and population. Instead of a summer cod fishery under command of a fishing admiral, English settlement had gradually led to permanent housing and the subsequent evolution of business and social activities. The town was described as 'looking more like a Yankee town' by the *Boston Journal* in 1866.

Our town of over 5,000 is now flourishing. Firms doing business include R.D. MacRae and Son, which has an enterprising fishery operation; W.A. Munn, manufacturers of cod liver oil; and Murray and Crawford, a seal oil operation. Those industries, along with the local fishery, are providing the amenities for more people to come here and live.

Imagine the first fishermen from Jersey who came here and fished the same waters we are fishing today. Their summer fishing activities were very similar to ours, except that they used Harbour Grace as a base rather than Harbour Grace Island. Cod is still the same species harvested, but there must have been more of them back then.

The first time I stood in the lighthouse, it was difficult for me to understand what was actually happening and why it was necessary to have a light and foghorn located on this remote island. Mr. Morris took the time to explain how the light operated and why lighthouses are important to help prevent accidents to ships and sailors at sea. It made me think about how important his job was compared to ours. Now when I see the light or hear the foghorn, I appreciate their presence more thoughtfully. We are glad to hear the groan of the foghorn ourselves on some days when we are out fishing and fog engulfs the area. It is a valuable beacon that serves to call us back to land.

While Fishermen's Island in summer is isolated, I often think about the light-keeper and his family who have to endure the harsher environment of winter in complete isolation and when stormy weather is more prominent. Frank and Fred would often tell me about a few of the storms they witnessed during their winters on Lighthouse Island when they were younger. It must take a particular kind of person to agree to subject himself and his family to a situation where the only social life is contained within your own family. However, many individuals and their families submit to the same obligations at many other lighthouse locations in Newfoundland and Labrador. I suppose they have a sense of pride in knowing they have a job that is intended to help prevent loss of life at sea and to facilitate marine transport. Notwithstanding those isolated positions, there must be some realization of importance and contentment that encourage light-keepers to assume such positions and accept the responsibility. Anyway, enough about Mr. Morris for now.

Fishermen's Island has a number of coves that have been given local names. The names are probably a reflection of someone's imagination, such as Devil's Cove and God Almighty Cove, or may denote a natural attribute, as can be seen in Sandy Cove, Gimlet's Cove, and Lobster Cove. All those names are like household words to me now that I have become a young fishing veteran of Harbour Grace Island.

A well-known landmark on the portside while steaming from town to Harbour Grace Island is Salvage Rock. The rock has weathered many a fierce storm, but still remains a guiding precipice to fishermen. Father uses it as a mark sometimes when we are fishing in order to locate a particular spot in which to start setting our fishing gear.

The fishing grounds that we use extend from Carbonear Island in the north to Feather Point in the south, although we sometimes venture beyond those boundaries. Our Island offers fishermen a location on which to build flakes and premises, all in close proximity to fishing grounds; this scenario is not possible if one is living in town. Bringing the whole family to the Island makes it a complete family fishing operation.

Yes indeed, it is May again and the winter is over, spring has arrived and the cod will soon be coming to shore, feeding on the abundance of capelin. We will also be there again on the fishing grounds to passively catch as much of the cod as is humanly possible with the manpower and fishing gear available. Every summer of fishing is viewed as a complete risk because we never know how much fish will be caught. Nevertheless, regardless of how bad last season's voyage has been, each new fishing season always seems to have an optimistic character to it; you prepare for the best, but often have to endure the worst.

My first day on the Island for this year is coming to a quiet end. What would this season bring? The start of this year is not much different for me, so far at least. Plenty of work for me today and most likely I will be kept busy tomorrow too. My fourteen-year-old frame is tested to the limit just trying to keep up with the older ones. How strong do they think I am?

I contemplate for a while and kindle my thoughts about where this kind of life will lead me. What are my other friends doing back in Harbour Grace? They certainly have more comfortable surroundings in town. One thing about the isolation of the Island is that it gives you plenty of time to think. However, you often have to do it while performing a chore of some kind.

The blackness of the night renders my eyes useless. I close them for a time and again let my mind wander. What would we encounter this summer? What would be different? What would be the same? Then a cool breeze jolts me as it wafts its way in through the door, and I shiver for a moment as my eyes spring open to bring me back to reality.

My tired young body now starts to yearn for some rest. Arms and legs ache from carrying load after load of supplies earlier in the day. Tiredness has brought early rest to most of my other family members, and I notice that quiet conversations have become fewer and fewer as sleep overtakes them. Even our dog Sport, has retired for the night. My sisters sought their beds earlier, and Walt is already asleep. Fighting sleep, I finally close the door on the rest of my world and settle down for the first night of sleep on the Island for the fishing season of 1922. This will be my fourteenth summer on the Island.

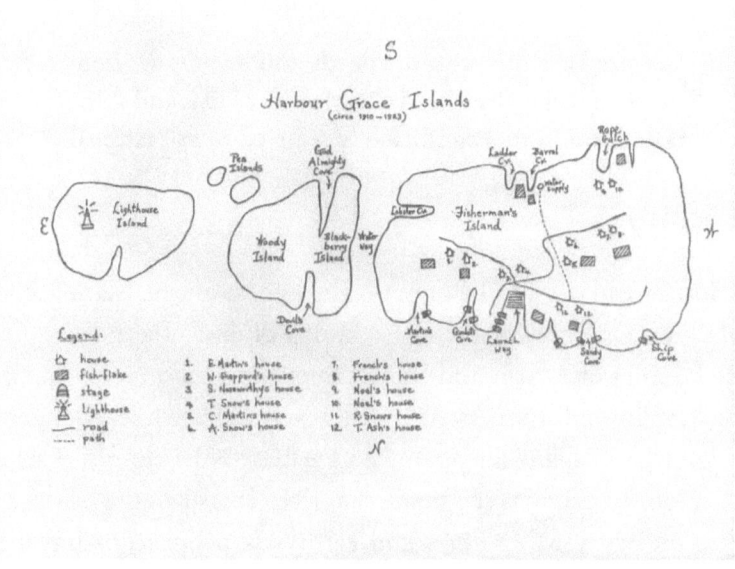

**Pattern of settlement on Harbour Grace Island
during the fishing season ca. 1910–23.
(Judy Finn)**

**Eviscerated codfish with the heads and backbones removed.
The pile is made by alternating layers of fish and salt. The
salted cod in this condition is referred to as "saltbulk."**

The Family

Mother said our family of ten is the largest on the Island, followed by Mr. Stewart Noseworthy, with a family of nine. There are eight each in the families of Austin and Robert Snow and John Noel. The family of Eli Martin and Thomas Ash have seven each, while Ebenezer and Silas French, William Sheppard, plus Albert Noel comprise six each. Mr. Charles Martin has the smallest at five. This gives the Island a total population of twelve families and eighty-six people; not much more than enough for a good Newfoundland scoff. However, considering that the demography of the Island consists of sixty-two offspring, the name of our Bay, Conception, is living up to its name.

My family consists of my parents, Thomas and Julia Ann, sisters Bessie (Bess), Lillian (Lill), and brothers William (Bill), Albert, George, Robert (Bob) and Walter (Walt). Missing now from our family is Winnie, who passed away on the Island in 1916 at only two years of age.

Mother and father came together after unfortunate incidents in previous marriages. An Englishman by the name of Chant had married mother. He was a seafarer, but maintained her in Halifax while he was away. However, word reached mother soon after he left on a voyage that he had died at sea after contracting a sickness. His family tried to persuade mother to come to England, but she decided to return home instead. Father's first wife had died leaving him with three boys, whom I refer to as my brothers. He and mother met and married and that marriage was followed by six more children, five of whom are living, including me of course.

Father is a brawny man with a conspicuous mustache and large sinewy hands. He goes about his business rather quietly and doesn't waste too many words. All the family treat him with respect and he is respectful of others. When I was about five years of age I would take great delight in putting on his big leather boots and parading around the kitchen, much to the delight of family members. His boots appeared so much bigger to me then, but not so much now.

Mother on the other hand is of smaller stature but still appears very capable in handling chores where strength is required. Her size doesn't hamper her but she always has a good knack of getting others to perform duties rather than doing them herself. Brain versus brawn as I have heard her say. Most times her long hair is tied in a bun. She always takes time whenever possible to speak with us and explain things, sometimes injecting a bit of humour. When I was a little younger I asked her, "Why do you have so much hair on your head?"

She replied, "Because I think a lot and that makes the hair grow."

She showed an impish smile when I then asked, "How come father's hair is really thin?"

Needless to say, we all have to make an effort to get along well together, and this results in not only much co-operation among our family members, but also among all Island residents. I believe too, even from my own somewhat immature observations, that the mere presence of a mother demonstrates a tremendous influence on the social well-being of family life on the Island. Family life and its values are the cogs that hold everyone together. We act as a unit and everything done by one often has an effect on us all. While husbands like my father have ups and downs brought about by the nature of his occupation, women like mother have an inherent ability to stabilize a situation.

Respect for each other is practised on a daily basis, and each year younger family members learn more and more as they mature and take responsibility for greater tasks. My case is no different, and I notice that each year more trust is put into my abilities. How simple it all is. A community of twelve families abiding with each other and having similar and mutual objectives. It appears that all we really have to do is obey the Ten Commandments. I admit there were occasions when I could have added a couple more commandments. While the Ten Commandments might not be broken very often, there are times when you could say they are badly bent. Like the time father and Mr. Stewart Noseworthy were lifting the stove and one leg happened to come down on father's toe. Well, I thought from the words coming out of father's mouth that Mr. Noseworthy had been given a new name that had a religious tone to it; so much for the Third Commandment.

I suppose our family life is typical of any fishing family. I certainly don't feel or look any different than my buddies. They have to do most of the same chores and complain about the same things as I do. Their complaints don't get much attention, either. As a result, we all just do as we are told to the best of our ability. Any time we step out of line, there is a quick reminder from the parents. Work comes first. There is a sense of preparation so that surprises are few. There's always something to do to prepare for the next day. "Never put off until tomorrow what you can do today." Now, that saying I have heard a few times from mother. I would be glad if they changed it to "Never do today what you can put off until tomorrow," but that is not going to happen.

The Next Day

Mother is up early to start our second day on the Island, and while very similar to the bustle of the first day, there is more a sense of permanence. We now complete the jobs on hand to firmly establish ourselves once again and prepare for the hard fishing season ahead. Father gives us orders regarding the strategy for the day from a fishing standpoint and mother takes care of everything else in and around the shack.

Not much of a life for a wife and mother after leaving the comfortable home we have in Harbour Grace and relegating herself to the rigours of existence here. Nonetheless, she appears to accept it as part of her married life; the words "for better or worse, richer or poorer" must demand the most from her. To me, being young of years, it all looks natural while watching my mother complete her daily rituals, but gradually it is taking on a new meaning. While the mothers on our Island do not actually participate in the action on the fishing boats, they certainly run a tight ship and keep everything sailing smoothly. And right now it is full steam ahead.

All day I work at several chores and begin to appreciate the saying, "a place for everything, and everything in its place." Father tells us where to put things in the various outside places, and mother knows where all items in the shack have to be placed. If I could describe our fishing situation on the Island as a ship, then father is the captain and mother the first mate. However, in regard to our fishing support operation, it can be classified as a mothership and there is no doubt who is the captain.

As the youngest of us grow older, more responsibility is correspondingly given. The oldest look after the youngest and in that way the youngest learn from the oldest. There is a definite sense of maturity becoming attached to my added responsibilities, and there are times I wish I were about eight years old again. I doubt whether the harder work is compensated by the realization and understanding that I have become more mature. What is this maturity bit anyway?

As I grow older, my life here on the Island experiences many changes. The youthful years seemed more like play rather than work because even though I helped with chores, I wasn't expected to accomplish very much. Now I am at the transition stage between boyhood and manhood. This is the period when I try to do a man's work in order to be called a man. My ego is really my own downfall. In trying to show my elders that I am a man, they further entice me by giving me more responsibility to go with it. There is no use pretending I can't do something once I have already done it. Do it once and you have to continue doing it! Father and the older boys encourage me to complete harder tasks because it lightens the load for them. Oh yes, it's a great feeling to be called a man.

Medical attention on the Island is really a family matter and mothers are the ones most often involved with accidents and sickness. Just this morning she had to remove a couple of wood splinters from the palm of my hand. We do not have any formal medical facilities and all injuries are treated in the best way possible. Broken bones or serious illness mean a trip to town for attention by the doctor. If bad weather prevents leaving, then we just have to wait.

Sometimes babies are born on the Island with the assistance of the midwife, Aunt Sophie Snow, who is also a resident here. Brother Bob was born here in 1906 and is the only one in our family to have that distinction. I don't know anything about it because he is two years older than I am. I have heard mother and father speak about it because it was intended that mother would go to town for the birth. However, a northeaster developed and leaving the Island was out of the question for about three days because of high winds and heavy seas. Bob was born the day the seas subsided. Luckily, there was no problem and Bob appears to be none the worst, but father often jokingly refers to him as a "real islander."

While comfort is given by Island families in times of trouble associated with birth, accident and death, such incidents are never forgotten. Memories linger on and stories often come up in conversation, some of which are happy while others are sad. In listening to family members discussing events in their lives over a cup of tea, it is clear that heartbreak, injury and loss are not far from the minds of many. It leads me to believe that they move on, but events are never forgotten.

Life Continues

Over the next few days all activities seem to take on a life of their own as each family gradually becomes settled in for another fishing year. Our summer home here on Fisherman's Island is a practical example of a traditional way of life. Subsistence flavoured with modest profit. My father is really an entrepreneur with his own capital investment and in charge of his own fishing enterprise. Most of all, he is his own boss. That is one thing not open to question. There is nobody going to tell him what to do (excluding mother, on occasion).

All family fishing enterprises now have their stages secured, slipways made ready and boats put in order for fishing. Yes, the objective of each and every fisherman from now on is to catch fish. This is the reason we are all here and our sole purpose for the next four to five months. Another year, another voyage.

Mother has seen to it that the shack also is readied. The very name "shack" certainly doesn't connote a place we would call home. It is very strange though, mother still demands we have a proper respect for the place. The building itself means nothing, it is the respect for family that makes it a part-time home. Someone once said it is the bricks and mortar that make a house, but the people inside determine the kind of home it will be. It is decidedly true in our case.

Shacks on the Island all look the same. Families are of equal status and nobody tries to impress another by building a better shack. A shack is a shack is a shack and is meant only to provide the basic necessities for supporting the fishing operations.

All shacks are basically of the same design, measuring about twenty-two feet long and fourteen feet wide. They are supported on crude rock foundations and floored with rough boards of spruce and fir. Outside walls are made from studs eight feet long and covered with felt. The rafters on the gable roof are fir or spruce with the rind removed, and made flat on the outside by chopping with an axe. The roof is covered with felt and tarred to make it waterproof. A copious amount of tar is used to try and prevent leaks. Felt is also applied to the outside walls.

The owners of a few shacks have clapboard applied to the front that has been mostly salvaged from re-clapboarding their houses in town. They use ochre and codfish oil on the clapboard to preserve the wood.

The inside partitions are made of boards nailed vertically side by side to the floor and secured on top to a wooden beam that extends across the width of the shack; this leaves an open space between the gable roof and the top of the partitions. Partitions and walls are papered with old newspapers including funny papers (comics) and catalogues. Each summer when we move to the Island, mother and the girls repaper the walls using paste made of flour and water, and this means I have new material at the beginning of each fishing season for my reading enjoyment. It helps to improve my reading and overall English skills.

The walls provide a measure of privacy but at the same time, the openness above them permits light and heat from the kitchen to penetrate through to other areas of the shack. Not that we have very much light except the kerosene lamps during the dark hours. On many a night I fall asleep reading the comic strips on the wall with the aid of a lamp. It is repetitious after a while but I get to know the comic strips very well and can even quote them.

Each shack has a window in the front and back and one in the largest bedroom. Needless to say, glass is not popular. Curtains on the windows are very rudimentary and most often are discarded curtains from home. The kitchen, which is indeed the largest and busiest area, measures roughly fourteen by ten feet and runs through the middle of the shack. It is the main room in the shack. Smack dab in the middle of the kitchen is the Ideal Cook stove which is fuelled with wood and used for both heating and cooking. There is no brick or mortar chimney, just funnelling that extends straight up and out through the roof. Where the funnel goes through the roof father makes it watertight by caulking around it with pug. This pug is made from cement-like mud found on the Island by digging down about one foot. It is then mixed with water to the consistency of putty before applying. Obviously it did the job well and at no cost. If a leak does develop, it is fixed by simply applying another batch of pug.

The only door for entrance to the shack leads into the kitchen. Then there are three bedrooms. Two bedrooms are on one end, one for us boys and one for the girls. On the other end is for want of a better word, the master bedroom and is the domain of my parents, but it also contains a small pantry; well, the pantry had to be somewhere.

Considering that I have five brothers, you can figure out for yourself the cramped sleeping arrangements. We all have bunks attached to the wall and mattresses stuffed with wood shavings. Although not as good as feathers, they are not too bad and they give a new meaning to contoured mattresses. Sometimes the wood shavings lump together, but a few manipulations with your hands usually correct the situation. We have to make the best of it because this is as good as it will get. Suffice to say, all of your waking hours are not spent lying down.

The kitchen is the hub of activity. I am amazed at mother, who is unfailing as she cooks meals, makes bread, sews clothes, and washes in the kitchen, while also making sure that the children, including me, are all looked after. Even on Sundays, when father has a break from fishing, she still does the cooking and generally cares for us. Now that I think of it, mother has that uncanny ability to be doing two or three manual jobs simultaneously, but yet be capable of giving verbal directions to some of us to perform other tasks. For example, she could be cooking dinner, folding clothes, and tending the stove and still have time to deal with us and explain things. Yet, some people have trouble with walking and chewing gum at the same time.

Furniture in the shack is crude or explicitly simple and most of it the result of manual labour. Handmade wooden benches, bunks and stools as well as the table, exemplify what I mean. Very little in the way of furniture is ever bought or even brought from town which makes shack life a complete and separate entity. There is no consideration or requirement to enhance our surroundings here on the Island beyond what is practical for our temporary stay. Neither is it considered financially feasible to expend large sums of money for short-term comfort. We are comfortable but not too comfortable. We all tend to appreciate what we have and realize the reason for it.

Moving to the Island means taking only items that will remain here or be used up by the end of the fishing season. Most items of use on the Island are purely practical and serve a useful purpose. A stool that we use is made from the stump of a tree. A dryer used for drying herring is carved from the trunk of a tree. Our grub-box in which we pack food to take out in boat while fishing was originally a butter tub. It has a liner made of sail-canvas to keep the food dry. There is also another wooden box lined with canvas and used to hold fish hooks and lead weights. Nothing considered of value is wasted and anything that can be made by hand is made that way.

Soundproofing inside the shack is not an option and complete privacy is difficult to accomplish. The activities of the workday often means early sleep for us younger ones. On occasion when sleep doesn't come early, we fuss about until a firm command from father gives us a definite indication that it would be in our best interest to find our bunks soon.

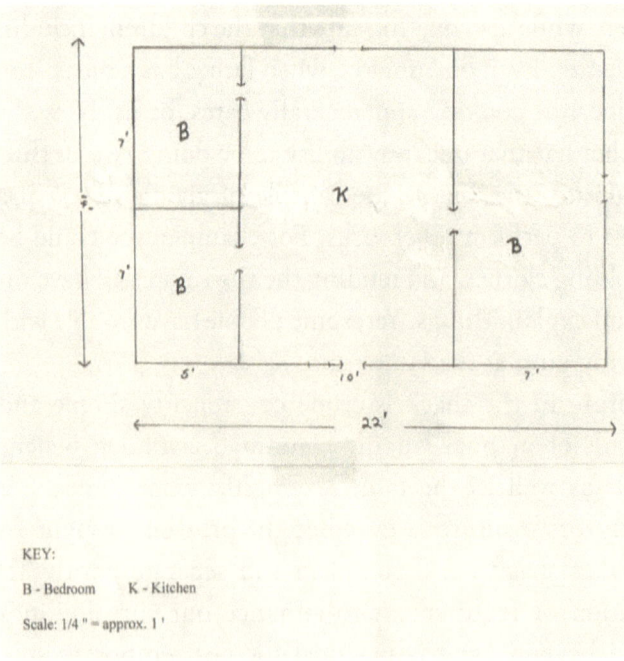

KEY:

B - Bedroom   K - Kitchen

Scale: 1/4 " = approx. 1 '

**Floor plan of the shack on Harbour Grace Island.
(Judy Finn)**

CHAPTER TWO

My Permanent Home

Our house in town is situated just off Noad Street. The street got its name from the man who designed and engineered the layout of Harbour Grace into blocks that consisted of two main streets and a series of cross-streets.

The house is a two-storeyed affair, facing south with dimensions of twenty-eight feet by eighteen feet and often referred to as a 'saltbox' design. It has a flat roof covered with felt and tarred to keep it waterproof; tarring is an annual chore. The flat roof means less material for construction and easy accessibility for repairs. Clapboard covers the outside and is painted cream-coloured with brown facings. The house has two brick chimneys, one running up through the kitchen and the other in the front room, which provides for a stove in each location. The front room has the most valuable furniture including an upholstered settee and hardwood table. Any handmade furniture is finished with wood stain or upholstered to give it a good appearance. Beds have feather mattresses and all floors are covered with canvas.

On the lower level of the house are the kitchen, a front room, a pantry and storage area for provisions. Father always makes sure we have enough of the basics like flour and sugar to last us throughout the winter. There is also a cellar in the storage area to keep vegetables safely from frost during the winter. We have another larger cellar close by as well on another piece of land that we own.

The back door leads into a porch, commonly called the 'backhouse,' that has only one small window. I suppose it got the name from the fact it is at the back of the house. The front door is a very solid design with a big lock and key. This door is used very infrequently, such as for special occasions, or if a stranger happened to come to the door by mistake. I have never used it. Inside this door and providing entry to the second level, is a set of stairs with a railing around the top. Nothing fancy about our house from a construction point of view although it serves its purpose well.

The second storey contains four bedrooms separated by a hall running through the centre. Each bedroom has its own bathroom consisting of toilet facilities under the bed (if you know what I mean) and a washstand with a large bowl and water jug. Small youngsters are usually given baths in large tubs set on the floor of the kitchen where hot water is readily available from a large galvanized pot on the stove; personal hygiene is something that I came to learn and respect. You have a full bath every week whether you need it or not. I'm past that stage now, but mother keeps tabs on me about cleanliness. I can hear her now: "Cleanliness is next to Godliness and don't forget to wash behind your ears!"

The kitchen is the main room in the house and it has a cast iron stove, canvas floor, couch, table and wooden chairs. The canvas on the kitchen floor is replaced every year because it wears through to the boards and is difficult to keep clean. Mother ensures it is replaced annually and selects the colour pattern. The kitchen is the area of most activity in the house. Consequently, it is usually painted each fall just before Christmas while other rooms in the house are painted as deemed necessary, and that is when mother requests it. Apart from a short period around Christmas when the front-room fire is lit, the kitchen is the only heated part of the house. Nevertheless, our home is a palace compared to the shack, and we are all obliged to treat it with utmost respect.

It is incumbent on the owner of each house to maintain the property. There is a sense of pride in keeping property in good condition and comparable at least to that of your neighbours. Any owner neglecting his property is treated with some disdain. As a result, the majority of houses and outbuildings in town are painted and well maintained. Fences are usually whitewashed. If premises are unkempt it can lower your social status and that is not an option for the majority of residents, certainly not father and mother.

Close to the house is the stable for Molly, our beautiful and capable black horse. Joined to it is the store that has a workbench and tools for doing many jobs. It also has a coal pound, a storage area for coal that we use during the winter. Father spends a lot of time in the store in the off-season repairing fishing gear and making repairs to anything that is broken. He also makes little wheelbarrows, cradles, and cots for younger ones. Sometimes I have known Father to spend a little longer than necessary in the store when he and mother are shall we say, having words.

It is in the store that I learn how to use carpenter's tools, sharpen an axe, make fish jiggers, mend twine, splice rope, and tie various knots. Those are the skills that I need to participate in the fishing operations on the Island and they often come in handy in other activities as well, whether it is on the Island or around home. Father passes on his own knowledge and this is also supplemented by skills learned from my older brothers. Every day is a learning experience. Tying knots may not seem important, but if it means securing a boat then it has importance. There are so many things to learn and none of it is written down, but passed on from older to younger in on-the-job training and in everyday life. The older I get, the more skills I acquire.

For a family like ours, we provide as much as possible for ourselves at the cheapest cost. Whatever the land and sea can provide we take advantage of it. We grow vegetables, cut our own wood, build and maintain our house, pick berries and bottle jams. Fish is a staple item of food and it comes easily because it is part of making our living. Father is also a good carpenter and mother can knit and sew clothes for all of us, especially the youngest. Calico (white coloured cotton cloth) flour bags are a popular material for making clothes. They are first washed to remove the printed pictures and wording of the particular brand of flour. This is not easy and sometimes the washing is not completely successful in doing the job. As a consequence one of our shirts could depict a 'Robin Hood' label in faded lettering. As a young boy I didn't mind it because I could play Robin Hood of Sherwood Forest complete with handmade bow and arrows.

Mother told me the story about the time she was present when father was counting out his small cache of gold pieces on the bed. When he turned his back she quickly took two pieces and slid them under the bed. Realizing he didn't notice they were gone, she knew her trick had worked. She spent the gold coins on a new fur coat for Lill and a sailor suit for me. To top it off, she had a photographer take our picture. This was one of the few times I had clothing bought at a store because most of my clothes were made by mother or were hand-me-downs. We did look cute in the new clothes and mother was proud of herself. I had a feeling father might have known, but what she had done pleased him too, so he kept quiet and enjoyed the moment.

Me in my sailor suit and Lill in her fur coat.

FLOOR PLAN OF OUR HOUSE IN HARBOUR GRACE

(Scale 1/4" = 2')

FIRST STORY

SECOND STORY

KEY:

F - Front Room	K - Kitchen	H - Hall	S - Storage
P - Porch	PY - Pantry	B - Bedroom	

Floor plan of our house in Harbour Grace.
(Judy Finn)

CHAPTER THREE

Fishing Thoughts

In the kitchens around the Island I can hear fishermen asking the same questions. I wonder how plentiful the cod will be this year? What kind of weather will we have this summer? What will be the price for salted fish this year? All those same questions are uttered each year and invariably the answers never turn out the same. No two seasons are alike. Although the cod make an appearance each year, there are some years when we catch far more fish than in others. I suppose there are reasons for it.

The most important ingredient for success is the presence of capelin. The abundance of those little fish is probably the contingent factor in our part of the ocean for a good fishing season. However, we can always count on their appearance each year between the 15th and 20th of June. Never in my family's memory have they failed to show up. As a matter of fact, I have never heard anyone even consider that capelin would not come to land. It is a traditionally annual occurrence.

Capelin exhibit a rather strange sort of behaviour during the spawning season, although not unlike certain other creatures in nature to ensure the continuation of the species. They seek out sandy beaches and the females lay their eggs on the rising tides. The males, readily distinguishable by distinct 'spawning ridges' along each side, are also close at hand to fertilize the eggs which then adhere to the sand. Sometimes the fertilized eggs (spawn) are six to eight inches deep in the sand. Many of the capelin die by becoming stranded on the beaches during the spawning process. The fertilized eggs are finally carried out to sea by the successive lowering tides to hatch and mature into adults.

My best coves for catching capelin include Sandy Cove and Sound Beach. Sandy Cove is very close to Thomas Ash's house, so if capelin are rolling onto the beach, he usually is the first to know. However, we sometimes have to row about one and one-half miles to Capelin Cove at the east end of Harbour Grace to replenish our capelin-bait supplies.

We also utilize capelin as a food by cooking them fresh or preserving them by salting and drying for later use. They provide us with a much-needed food supply as well as a bait fish for hand-lines in our fishing operations. Capelin are a favourite prey for other fish species, marine mammals and birds. Cod, salmon, gulls, puffins, gannets, seals, whales and porpoises are all predators. I have watched whales and birds prey on them. Capelin are also used as a cheap form of fertilizer by burying them into the ground and letting them rot naturally. We use them in our gardens here on the Island and also in our gardens in Harbour Grace.

The cast-net is the method we mainly use to catch capelin. The bottom part of the net contains lead balls that permit it to sink quickly when released. Using a capelin cast-net is a completely manual operation and requires some dexterity and coordination. It is done by taking the net and putting a part of the lower end in your teeth and that keeps it high and helps to spread the net. Then you take the remaining lower part in your hands and spread your arms apart. When the school of capelin are within range, you swing your arms backward to obtain force and then forward again while at the same time releasing the net from your hands and teeth. This requires tremendous skill when casting from a boat bobbing on the waves or from slippery rocks in a cove. When released, the cast-net fans out over the capelin. It can also be tricky for someone with false teeth. As the net sinks over the capelin, they become trapped inside until hauled ashore or into the boat.

Brothers Bill and George are very adept at using this piece of technology. They have acquired the knack from father who let them try it when capelin were plentiful. It takes considerable practice to become proficient and maybe even getting wet a few times. I found out that it is very important to release your hands at the precise moment, if not you could follow the net overboard. Bill and George have both become capable individuals and do not appear to find even the most strenuous and demanding tasks very difficult. On occasion they take delight in it.

The Fishing Operation

It may be difficult for anyone not associated with life on the Island to envisage our working environment. Consequently, I will try with my still limited knowledge to provide basic information to increase appreciation and instil a better understanding of our summer fishing residence and fishing establishment.

The harvest of cod is our main concentration even though other species are also taken. For over 400 years the cod species has been the main reason for the existence of settlement here in Conception Bay. John Cabot, after discovering Newfoundland in 1497, mentioned that cod were so plentiful they could be dipped up in baskets. This may have been an easy exaggeration, but in some years they are very plentiful and can be seen swimming near the surface of the water when chasing and gorging themselves on capelin. I have never tried to dip them up in a basket or even a dip-net.

How peaceful and pristine everything must have appeared to John Cabot when he first sighted land off Cape Bonavista. He also most likely glimpsed the Great Auk, a somewhat penguin-like bird that became extinct after Europeans arrived. It was a man-made extinction like others I have read about. I suppose the need for food overcame any consideration for conservation of those large birds. What a shame they are no more.

When Cabot returned to England and told about the abundance of fish, a wave of new adventurers showed up off our shores. The Grand Banks of Newfoundland were visited by fishermen from many countries, including Spain, Portugal, France, and Norway, and of course England. Fishermen were not permitted to settle in Newfoundland on a year-round basis until well after the first colony was established in Cupids, Conception Bay, in 1610. The first captain to arrive from England each year became the fishing admiral for that season. He set his own rules and in some respects could be classified as a fishing dictator or, more respectably, the fishing administrator. The name would depend on the attitude displayed by each of the fishing admirals. The captains of ships returning to England with holds full of salted cod were welcomed with fanfare and rewarded generously.

During the latter 1600s when more fishermen began to take up permanent residence, fishing activities evolved into towns and villages that soon dotted the coast. Each fisherman tried to find the most suitable cove or harbour from which to carry out fishing operations. Squatters' rights were entrenched and every fisherman respected each other's territory. Fishermen who settled in Harbour Grace split up the available shoreline into 'rooms,' as they called them. Gradually those rooms evolved into private ownership and land rights. For my ancestors, coming to these shores did not really mean leaving their country because Newfoundland was part of the Empire. They just adventured here to pursue the same fishing trade, but anticipated it would be more lucrative. In effect, they were fishing pioneers.

The Grand Banks became known as a very prolific fishing area, probably because it is a vast shoal relatively speaking, and it lies at the interception point between the cold Labrador Current and the warm Gulf Stream. However, this also causes severe foggy conditions as well. I heard one old fellow say jokingly that John Cabot was within sighting distance of Newfoundland two days before he actually sighted it on June 24. It was just too foggy to see it.

I mentioned that fishermen took up locations as close to the fishing grounds as possible. Our migration to Fisherman's Island each summer is for that same purpose and it serves as our temporary home; a home away from home, just as European fishermen came to Newfoundland years before to fish during the summer. While the Island gives us fishing advantages, there are many disadvantages of a social nature that we have to endure to reap the fishing benefits. Proximity to the fishing grounds is however, the utmost consideration for any prudent fisherman and father is one of them.

Fishermen over the years have designated specific fishing areas around the Island. In this way, every fishing enterprise has their own area to fish and there is consensus as to where those areas are located. There are still certain fishing grounds not designated and all enterprises can fish there, especially during certain times of the year. Father says that it is all done by what he calls 'gentlemen's agreement.' The skippers of fishing enterprises often share knowledge and if cod are plentiful in one area, it's not uncommon to see a number of boats fishing in that area. Sharing is commonplace.

The designated areas for fishing have been handed down over generations and probably developed by trial and error until it became evident that certain areas were more likely to be the preferred places to catch cod. Specific names are given to those fishing areas, such as Black Rock, White Rock, Ragged Rocks, Eastern Rock, and Sandy Ground. I am beginning to know them all myself. Each of those areas is delineated by visual sightings in at least two directions that intersect one another. For instance, a fishing area could be located by picking a spot on Carbonear Island and then having it intersect with the Lighthouse in Harbour Grace. A lot of judgment is involved and the marks for each fishing area have to be committed to memory. I don't have to worry about committing them to memory now, but obviously my older brothers have acquired the knowledge. Since it's all based on memory, the only way to learn is to have someone tell you.

A compass is sometimes used in addition to visual aids to ensure we are in the exact fishing area or spot. The compass is another gadget I know I have to master in the future. I already know the main points of the compass. Father has explained to me a little about how it works. I know that the needle points to the magnetic north all of the time but I still don't know why. Must be quite a magnet at the North Pole to cause a needle to point north way down in Harbour Grace. It seems fun for me sometimes finding our way back to the Island when it becomes foggy. Of course father has to know what direction to take, and I can only assume he has also committed that to memory. I haven't seen him mark down anything.

The areas that we fish also depend in many cases on the time of year. We often fish areas in the early fall different from those we fish during midsummer. It appears as if the skippers of fishing enterprises know from years of experience that cod move to different places with the seasons. Oh there is so much to learn in this business that is not written in books. I continue to learn from watching, listening, and asking questions, but not too many questions, especially when things are not going favourably. On days when fishing is good I can ask father anything, but when fishing is not good my questions are few.

Permit me now to describe the various parts of our fishing operation that are similar to most others on the Island. First of all, consider our fishing boat and fish-catching equipment. Our main boat is a large punt, twenty-four feet long and used for all major fishing operations. It carries nets, traps, and trawls to the fishing grounds and brings the fish back to the landing site on the Island. This is our 'bread and butter' boat, so to speak. I can picture this fishing craft in my mind with her spanker billowing in the wind as we tend our trawls late in the season. Yes, she is a sturdy craft that father made with the help of a few other men from cut timbers with planking nailed to them and caulked with oakum before being covered with white paint. Rowed with two oars, she is not an easy boat to propel when loaded with fish. Sometimes a 'sculling oar' is used to augment the rowing. This special oar is inserted out through a hole in the stern well above the waterline and propels the boat through a series of rolling and paddling movements, both conducted at the same time. A peg is inserted at the top part of the oar handle to allow the user to perform the rolling action with one hand while paddling with the other. I don't mind sculling when the weather is good, but in a breeze I am content when someone else offers to take on the task. In certain situations, it is better to let wits overcome brawn especially when any brawn I have is not readily distinguishable.

Hand-lines are our most important pieces of fishing equipment, although the Noels and Frenches use cod traps more extensively. We have only one small cod trap. The cod trap is an ingenious device supposedly developed by Captain William H. Whitely in the late 1860s while fishing off Labrador. Its fishing success depends on one very well-known phenomenon peculiar to many free-swimming fishes. That is, when fish are swimming adjacent to the shoreline and encounter some obstruction, they naturally turn toward the sea. The cod trap is designed, constructed, and set to take advantage of that inherent trait. This is a truly innovative method of fishing even though it catches only the cod that happen to be passing by.

There are other pieces of fishing gear apart from the hand-lines that comprise our fishing paraphernalia. These include gillnets for herring, mackerel and salmon; longline-trawls for cod, flounder, and other types of bottom-dwelling species; cast nets for capelin; jiggers for cod and jiggers for squid. Hand-lines take different forms as well. For instance, we use dabbers with capelin as bait to catch cod during the capelin season. Later in the season we use baited hooks with a lead weight attached because fish are then feeding on the bottom. Another trick is to also use our salmon net as a gill-net for cod. The difference is that instead of setting it on the surface, as we do for salmon, it is set on the bottom.

Although we set our salmon net in the summer, the capture of salmon is only for food for the family. We do not usually catch very many, but those we do catch are most often eaten immediately or salted for later consumption. We catch between ten and twenty each summer. Atlantic salmon are beautiful-looking fish and very lively when taken from the net. They are prized as a food item and a meal of salmon is considered a treat. I think it is too, and I wish there were more of them.

Conception Bay is not known to produce too many salmon, but I have heard that in years past there were more. Two small brooks at the bottom of our harbour originally had runs of salmon, but they may have been fished out after permanent settlement occurred. It is probably true because I sometimes catch young salmon in Lady Lake. Knowledgeable people told me they are landlocked salmon and no longer go to the sea. The dam placed at the river outlet from Bannerman Lake probably disrupted the salmon migration process because Lady Lake runs into Bannerman Lake. I have read stories of salmon angling in Scotland in our school books. Father told me the salmon we catch are headed to rivers around other areas of Newfoundland to spawn.

Lobster fishing is not part of our regular fishing activity, at least not for commercial use. We do take advantage of our knowledge of the area to secure a few lobsters for our own eating enjoyment. I have a nice, long pole with a hook on it for that purpose and call it my lobster-pole. My buddy Ron Ash and I row in to Feather Point and drop some fish guts down alongside a few large rocks and wait. There are no lobster pots set in this location, so we are not interfering with anyone's fishing activity. As soon as a lobster crawls out from under the rocks to eat the fish, I push my pole down and hook it. With any luck, we can get three or four lobsters this way. I certainly don't take them all because every year I can come here and hook a few and they are usually two pounds and more in weight. Lobsters are not really plentiful in our area, but a meal of them every now and again pleases Ron and me. We make a fire outside to boil them in mother's big cast-iron pot and share them mainly with the smallest children.

Apart from the actual fishing apparatuses, there are structures that play an integral part in our operation. One of those is the stage. This flimsy looking building provides the transition between water and land, a sort of marine complex built over the face of the shoreline. This is where we land and discharge our fish catches for later processing. It is also our fish-processing facility. The stage is constructed to permit boat access and to provide a shelter for the fish while it is curing. It is also a storage area for much of the equipment and utensils used in our day-to-day operations. Come to think of it, father spends a great deal of his time in and around the stage when he is not on the water because it is the hub of fishing activity. Our stage is adjacent to those of Mr. Austin Snow and Mr. Robert Snow.

The floor of the stage is built of longers, small spruce or fir tree-trunks about ten feet long, that rest on 'shores,' which are nothing more than spruce pilings. The roof rafters are also made of spruce or fir and covered with sods to make the place waterproof. Walls are of spruce or fir boards. The quality of our fish is of utmost concern to father. Therefore, over the fish-curing area on both sides of the stage, father nails up felt to protect the fish from roof drippings during rain. Father contends that if we bring good-quality fish to the buyer, it will be very difficult for the buyer to justify giving a low price. Lower fish quality usually means lower prices from the buyer.

Housed in the stage is a spare of everything that might break or wear out during the season. Father has to be proficient at everything from fixing the boat to repairing the shack. If a repair job requires more than one adult or some specific skill, there is usually someone on the Island who volunteers to help and we learn by watching. Trial and error is a way of life for me.

This past winter severe damage was done to the stage by ice and rough seas that took us about a week to repair. Father, Albert, and Bob had to make two trips to Harbour Grace to get extra sticks for this repair job.

Following our return from the Island last fall, father told me that I would be responsible for looking after the cod livers this year. We brought two empty beef barrels to the Island for that purpose. I placed them next to the stage. I will now have to collect all the livers after the cod are gutted and place them in the barrels. The livers will 'render out,' and raw cod-liver oil will remain. At the end of the season the cod-liver oil will be sold to W.A. Munn for refining into a drinkable form for human consumption. According to one of my teachers, codfish build up Vitamin D in their livers and drinking it improves our health. It is the same Vitamin D that we get from the sun. Hard to imagine how a cod liver can be linked to the sun. In any event, mother ensures we have a spoonful every day in the winter so there must be some truth to it. Even though it is refined, it still has an unwelcome taste, but we all grin and bear it as we grimace during each spoonful. My sisters are not keen on it at all and it takes all their willpower to swallow the stuff.

Producing salt fish is the process of washing, salting and drying. When the cod are landed they are first gutted (eviscerated), headed, split (most of the backbone removed and the tail section cut so that the fish can lie flat), washed thoroughly in salt water, and then covered with salt. In our case, the fish are salted, some in puncheons or barrels that retain the liquid. Father considered this a better method because all the fish in each container are immersed in the pickle which provides more uniformity in the curing process. There are many skills associated with this whole operation, especially in the splitting process. It requires manual dexterity, especially when using the razor-sharp knife on slippery surfaces. Workmanship is key to producing a good-quality product because round-tails (tails not properly split) and rough textured surfaces lower the quality and price. Father exhibits much care and pride in having the best quality, and my brothers follow his example

I have tried my hand at splitting cod but have not yet mastered the task. George and Bill have perfected the process and Albert has just about met perfection, but father notices a few glitches now and then. I'm not too anxious to take over from them. I'm content to just pass them the fish for gutting, heading and splitting. My day will come soon enough.

Heavy-salted and light-salted are the two main types of cures and refer to the amount of salt used. We produce heavy-salted product. Heavy-salted fish requires about 40 lbs. of salt/100 lbs. of fish, and light-salted about 10 lbs. salt/100 lbs. Heavy-salted fish must remain in salt or pickle for twenty-one days. During the curing process the salt replaces the water in the fish and acts as the preservative. In academic terms, it refers to the process of osmosis that I learned in school last year. I remember looking up the word osmosis in the dictionary. However, it is not a word I hear used very often on the Island, even though we are surrounded by it. We take the scientific explanation for granted and don't worry ourselves about the actual process. The practical aspects are what's important and not the theory.

After the fish are cured and washed, there is one final part of the process that requires us to have a drying mechanism. We use 'flakes.' No, they have nothing to do with breakfast cereal, but rather are structures used for the natural drying of our fish. Here on the Island we are usually blessed with a breeze that makes it quite suitable for fish drying. Sun-dried fish we call them. The flakes are nothing more than poles nailed horizontally to beams that are all supported by bigger shores to keep them about seven feet off the ground. The height of the flakes also allows people to walk under them when moving from one part of the Island to another. The wind can thus circulate above and below the fish to combine with the sun's heat to do the drying. The tops of the flakes are covered with spruce boughs on which the fish are laid or spread. It is a simple but effective drying process. You could call it a solar dryer.

All of the wooden material for the flakes and other items comes from wood cut in the forests to the north of the town and generally around Lady Lake. Molly is used to haul this wood on a sled during the winter season to our house. It's quite a sight to see all the horses, including Molly, with loads of wood coming down over Kitchen's Hill about midday. Wood is very important for many practical purposes as I can see within our household and in fishing operations.

We even brought firewood to the Island because the landscape here is basically bare except for a few shrubs. The cost to obtain wood by our family is not a factor as our own labour is used. All we have to do is cut, saw and dry it.

CHAPTER FOUR

Work in Town

The cooler breezes of early spring gradually change to become warmer and softer as May fades into June. The land heats more rapidly each day with the sun and that often means the creation of sea breezes from an easterly direction, which are common during this time of year and frequently occur during the whole summer. We know that summer is approaching because on warm afternoons mother lets the stove 'go out' for a couple of hours to save our wood fuel. Since wood has to be brought from town, it is incumbent on her to conserve as much as possible to ensure we have enough to get through the fishing season.

The warmth also brings with it additional chores in Harbour Grace, for it is time to prepare our vegetable gardens. It is also an opportunity for me to get to town to see many of my friends again. Seed we plant will provide us with the harvest of vegetables needed for the coming winter. These are mainly potatoes, carrots, beets, turnips, and cabbage. Manure from the stable suffices for fertilizer, compliments of our horse Molly, and our goats Daisy and Rosie.

We have a number of gardens in town, and each is designated by the crop grown in it. Thus, we have a potato garden, a cabbage garden, and most often, more than one hay garden. We also cut the hay and dry it in gardens owned by other residents. It is done by mutual agreement, whereby they get their grass cut and we get the hay with no money changing hands.

Plenty of hay is needed to feed Molly, Daisy and Rosie throughout the winter and early spring. Much of the hay is stored in our overhead loft above the barn and store. A hinged door leads from the loft down to the barn for easy access to the hay. Feeding the animals is usually one of my jobs before I leave for school.

Chopping wood is another of my fall chores. The wood that father had cut the previous winter is dry by the fall and ready to cut and split for firewood. George, Albert, Bob, and I do most of the cutting and piling of wood. My main job is carrying the wood into the store and stacking it to protect it from rain and snow in order to keep it dry. We also pile a quantity against the store and cover it with canvas. We have to have enough wood for the house and also for the next fishing season on the Island. The amount of wood used at the house depends on the relative harshness of the winter. Supplemented by coal, we always have enough.

Often I ride down with father to Munn and Company for a load of coal using our horse and box-cart. Molly doesn't appear to have any trouble hauling the box-cart full of coal back home. Father dumps the coal next to the door leading into the store. It is then my job to shovel the coal into our coal-pound, and that is messy. Coal dust spreads everywhere and my face is usually black when the job is finished.

Molly is a strong animal and has the capacity to undertake many chores. In the winter, she hauls wood and also provides horsepower for those particularly wonderful sleigh rides. It is tremendous fun riding on the sleigh. Father keeps a piece of canvas stretched across the two forward horns of the sleigh to stop the snow kicked up by the horse's hooves from hitting us in the face. This canvas becomes even more useful if Molly decides to relieve herself while in full trot. I sometimes ask friends along and they never refuse.

In late spring, Molly is used for ploughing and hauling cargo of many kinds. However, during the summer while fishing is underway, she has a break and is free to roam with the other horses and graze on the hillsides. When fall arrives she ploughs up potatoes and hauls coal and vegetables plus other cargo, such as fishing gear, to storage. There is no doubt about it, she earns her keep.

We have various pieces of equipment to use with Molly, such as the 'dray' for general cargo, plus the 'hay-frame' that can be attached for hauling hay; the 'box-cart' for loose cargo such as coal; the 'slide' for wood; the 'sleigh' for passenger travel in winter; and the 'plough' used for preparing the gardens for planting and harvesting. The value of our horse, Molly, is preeminent. I sometimes ride her bareback as well.

We all have a good appreciation for animals. Although we regard them as necessary for part of our livelihood, there is a certain satisfaction in being around them. Molly in particular certainly knows who is kind to her. She has learned to know who treats her the best and who the worst. There is a subtle grey area between showing her who is in command and treating her with respect. You have to know where to draw the line between kindness and authority. She is attuned to the treatment received from those who work with her and treats them accordingly. Molly's importance to us makes her basically one of the family, so father and the rest of us know her limits and do not push her beyond her endurance. She likes to get special treatment and relishes the occasional treat of oats. Perhaps her favourite treat is the liquor left in the pot after mother cooks pork and cabbage dinner and that she can count on every week.

While in an animalistic frame of mind, I must tell you about our two seafarers, Rosie and Daisy. These are our two milking goats that accompany us to the Island each year. When the time comes to set sail for the Island, Rosie and Daisy are ready to hop right into the punt and ardently look forward to the voyage. They sit quietly in the boat among all the supplies with only the very infrequent 'ma, ma, ma' as if to confirm their enjoyment of the ride. Having made the voyage before, they seem to relish the trip each year and never give us any problems. Therefore, they too, have become an integral part of our summer fishing-migration and a good source of fresh milk.

Back on the Island

Our time in town is short-lived, and after a two-and-one-half-hour boat trip I am once again subjected to the rigours of the Island. While on the Island, we supplement our food supplies with produce that can grow during the late spring and summer. Each family has at least one small garden. Since there is no official ownership of the land, each family picks and chooses a piece to use for growing crops. Once chosen, the piece of land is crudely fenced before the planting is done.

Gardens are selected so that one side faces a cliff and that reduces the amount of fencing required. Fences are usually in a semicircle. They are needed to keep out the roaming goats and dogs. All families grow enough vegetables to maintain them during the late summer, and as vegetables mature, they are eaten.

Rhubarb is one of the earliest crops to harvest, and mother does a good job of converting it into pies and jam. Except for fixing up the rhubarb beds each year, it really grows wild. The limited amount of soil on the Island is put to good use.

Very soon I am beckoned to help sow the crops, knowing full well my mother and sisters will tend them during the growing season. However, it is Albert's, Bob's, and my job now to put the fences in place This work is relatively easy for me, but I soon get to learn that the more I become capable of doing, the more I am given to do.

I help my older brothers and they give me the easiest jobs to do. It is fun to plant and sow seed and then watch the plants grow into fine vegetables. As we work, I look forward to harvest time and the taste of fresh crops. We use prongs and shovels to till the soil.

Around the Island other families have set out their gardens and put up fences. From the air, the fencing must look like a patchwork because everything from sticks to old pieces of netting are used; the easiest and cheapest items we can find to do the job. However, fences are for the most part made from small sticks or pickets with the bark left on them.

As boys, we all learn by watching and observing. The ego in us makes us try new things and each of us want to succeed. There is a lot of pride in doing a chore for the first time and many of us grow up really fast.

Within a few days, we are subjected to 'capelin weather,' so called because every year during the arrival of capelin, the weather is foggy with an easterly wind. The wind blows the fog toward the land, especially during late afternoon and night. We are usually so busy during this time in June that weather is not even a consideration as long as we have a compass, and father always ensures we do.

Most fishermen by this time are becoming anxious and can't wait to start hand-lining. As mentioned, the Frenches and Noels are the only crews using mainly cod traps. We have already gone out in the boat a few times and tried the cod-jigger at various places to find out if any fish are around. The last time out we caught enough to fill the forward pound in the punt.

Cod jigging is not easy when you are at it for a number of hours, for it requires constant movement to keep the jigger operating properly. Although there is a certain enjoyment in catching fish, the more you catch the less enjoyment because then it becomes hard work.

The frequent meals of fresh-fried cod make the effort worthwhile and I clean out my plate most times rather quickly to await seconds. I am treated to many meals of cod during the season, as you can appreciate. We will have fried fish, stewed fish, cod tongues, fish peas, rounders, fish and brewis, and salt fish with drawn butter. If fish is a brain food, the top of my head will have bumps on it. Time to call it a night.

CHAPTER FIVE

The Cod Are Here

Daylight comes early, and I am up and out in the boat with the rest of our crew before four-thirty a.m. We set sail along with other crews, with our fresh capelin bait for the hand-lines. There is a calmness as George rows the boat through the fluorescent water, and only the rubbing of the oars against the toll-pins breaks the silence of the coming dawn. We approach the shoal quietly and lower the grapnel. Capelin are secured on the hooks, two per man except for father, who operates three lines, one on each side of the boat and one over the stern

Very soon I can see the mid-ship-room in the boat starting to fill with cod. There is a good feeling that you get when the cod start to bite and you know the day is going to be successful. We are all busy as we tend our lines without too much in the way of conversation. I take a minute to observe the different colours of the fish that range from reddish to black on their backs before becoming white on the stomachs. I ask father why the fish vary in colour on their backs. He ponders just a short while as he removes another fish from his hook and says, "The colours stem from the food they eat and the type of bottom where they live."

I can't think of a better explanation right now.

Today the average size of the cod is about twenty-four inches. Cod fishing often produces much variability in fish size, but we all contend that in this catch it is not as noticeable. Father surmises, "These are probably the cod that stayed closer to shore and in the Bay during the past winter rather than the cod that normally follow the capelin. I expect that will soon change."

After fishing for about six hours, the frequency period of cod on our lines is becoming farther and farther apart. Only the odd one is being taken and it looks like they have 'struck off' for the day. Father sizes up the situation and decides it is time we headed for home to gut and split our catch. While this trip of about five quintals is not extraordinary, it indicates a good omen for the days ahead.

Since we have only an average catch, I am left to prong the fish from the boat to the stage. It isn't too difficult today because the tide is high and the gunnels of the boat are close to the top of the stage-head. Bob and Albert get the splitting table ready and father and Bill begin the gutting and splitting process. George fills the puncheon tub with water for washing the split fish. I later help with the washing and then George says, "Make sure all the blood and pieces of liver are completely removed," as I go about the task.

There is no shortage of water because we use the ocean, and we have no worry of that well running dry; it is cold, too.

The draw-bucket we use is a subtle device for getting water. It consists of a metal bucket with a rope tied to the handle. All I have to do is drop the bucket overboard, give a quick jerk to flip it over, and let it fill with water before hauling it up with the rope. With the high tide I don't have far to haul it, which makes this job a lot easier.

After the fish receive a good washing, Bob and Albert place them down in the puncheons and sprinkle solar salt over them; a layer of fish and then a layer of salt. The first major fish curing event of the season is under way and we anticipate repeating it many more times.

Father told me that the solar salt we use comes from the Mediterranean Sea or the Caribbean. Our teacher told us it is obtained by trapping saltwater in shallow pools and letting it evaporate until only the salt is left. Must be a lot warmer there than it is here for that to happen. I have seen big ships come into Harbour Grace with loads of salt. Also, vessels that transport fish to Spain, Portugal, Italy, and the Caribbean Islands often bring back salt cargoes.

As I am becoming older, it is obvious that in order to survive and subsist in our way of life you have to make full use of everything available to you. Such is the case with the cod that we catch. In preparing the cod for salting, we remove the guts and heads before cutting out most of the backbone. We then remove the eyes and gills from the heads before salting them for our own use. The chitlins (male organs) and roe sacs (female eggs) are also removed, washed, and salted, as are the air sacs (swim bladders or sounds). The only parts of the cod discarded are the gills, backbones, eyes, and guts. The female cod we catch in the fall have better roe sacs because then the roe is more ripe.

Sometimes we cut the tongues from the heads and mother fries them in her cast-iron frying pan along with small pieces of fatback pork. I love them, but so do most everyone else in the family. There is a knack to cutting out the cod tongues, but I mastered that technique a few years ago.

Mother cooks the salted cods' heads by sometimes baking them in the oven in a sort of stew. They are delicious and I can taste the juice from them now. Sucking on the bones and crunching up the cartilage makes it one of my favourite meals. Yes sir, a few cods' heads along with boiled potatoes and homemade bread is a meal hard to beat for us sea-farers, but probably doesn't have the same connotation for landlubbers.

Another Day

I often stand on the Island during a foggy day and marvel at the effect this naturally produced vapour has on the surroundings. It is uncanny how fog changes the visual landscape to a grey blur. It is akin to going blind. No longer can I see the land to the north, south, and west of me, but I can still hear some of the sounds, including the foghorn on Lighthouse Island. Many times, the sounds appear to be louder, as if the fog were carrying them like a conductor. Occasionally, I can witness the onset of the fog as it gradually comes in through Conception Bay until it finally engulfs the Island. It tends to add a more enclosed feeling to my already isolated existence by shutting out everything around me. It sort of gives the impression that we are the only people in existence.

On this one particular day, the easterly wind is accompanied by rain and a large undertow. No fishing is taking place so the boats are secured. Father had predicted this weather the day before it happened. It seems to me quite amazing how he can just stand outside the shack, look at the sky, and predict the future weather. Other fishermen have the same abilities because my friends often give me their fathers' forecasts. This is a gift handed down from generation to generation and based on information not often found in books. In pursuing a living through fishing, weather is important, and fishermen tend to study the skies and make mental notes that gradually lead to anecdotal descriptions of their own. Signs like mackerel sky, ring around the sun and ring around the moon, red sunset and red dawning have particular meanings. Sea conditions like strong currents and ocean stillness also play a part in local weather forecasting. Of course, fishermen on the Island do not always agree with one another concerning the predictions of oncoming weather. This sometimes leads to very good dialogue among them. Most times consensus is reached after it is all said and done, but not always.

Father can argue with the best of them, but Mr. Tommy Ash is probably the 'king of the Island' in that department. He has the ability to analyze what others say and then make a pronouncement that is a mixture of the views of the others and therefore, not open to much contradiction. He is often referred to as an armchair lawyer by some of the other fishermen. He also has a great ability to stir up an argument by just injecting a simple statement and then sitting back with a sly grin on his face and calmly listening to his fishing colleagues as they argue. There is often a lot of humour associated with some of these episodes. It sounds like a lot of fun, and I often try some of Mr. Tommy Ash's techniques on my friends.

I have heard many stories told by fishermen and sailors who sailed to fishing grounds offshore or to lands across the Atlantic, many of them involving foggy conditions. It is quite a feat to leave port in fog and be capable of finding distant fishing grounds. What's even more fantastic is being able to find your way back. Stories have been told about particular skippers who seem to possess qualities that make them good navigators in fog and in storms. I have heard the men refer to it as 'dead reckoning.' I suppose that means if you reckon right, you are okay, and if not you are dead.

Something tells me I'd better get back to my chores or I might meet the same fate. I don't want to provoke father into doing something to my detriment.

These types of days are anything but pleasant here on the Island. The gloominess of the weather, coupled with the stoppage in fishing activity, provides a real contrast to our usual routine. Yet everyone seems to have something worthwhile to do. In most cases, we do the things we don't get a chance to do on a busy fishing day.

Bob and I help out with rearranging some of the fish in the stage to try and give us a little more room. George is kept busy bringing water from the well. Bill and Albert are strengthening the flakes in anticipation of future good catches of cod. Father is generally supervising all that is happening, barking out some command every now and again and splicing rope at the same time.

Although we are not fishing today, mother, Lill, and Bessie are still busy, and their ongoing work continues. For them every day is alike, regardless of the weather. However, since we are all ashore today, they are able to coax us into helping them with some of their usual chores.

Fishing Is Interesting

Very often when fishing during midsummer we encounter dolphins, and it is interesting to see them swimming around our boat in pursuit of capelin. During one such occasion, I decided to try and catch one of them. I put two capelin on my hook, threw it as far as I could from the boat and waited. Knowing the dolphins would exert a good weight on the line, I tied the end to the boat. I threw out the line several times and each time waited and waited, but the dolphins did not take the bait. However, they were still swimming around our boat chasing the capelin. I finally hauled in my line, took the capelin off the hook and threw them overboard. As soon as the capelin hit the water a dolphin surfaced and ate them. This set me thinking. I took a couple of more capelin and tossed them overboard only to see another dolphin rise to the surface for them.

Thinking I might now be able to catch one, I again put two capelin on my hook and tossed the line from the boat, but to my chagrin the dolphins did not take the bait. I hauled in my line once more, removed the two capelin and tossed them overboard, only to see a dolphin appear and gulp them down again.

Obviously dolphins have developed enough brainpower to know that bait on the end of a line is not normal and therefore it is not to be eaten. Father, George, and Albert were getting some pleasure from watching me trying to catch the dolphins, and that probably indicated they had tried the same before and were only letting me go through the process to learn for myself.

"Probably you should try putting *three* capelin on your hook," said George in a humorous tone that brought smiling reactions from Father and Albert.

They wanted to make the most of this charade, but I had already concluded that catching a dolphin in this way was not going to happen.

It looks as if the dolphins' intelligence is above my innovative technique for trying to catch them. Since that experience, I am content to just throw the capelin overboard and watch them come to the surface. I enjoy their presence now without trying to test their mental capabilities.

We encounter many other creatures while fishing, especially during the capelin season. Frequent visitors are humpback whales. They often swim close to our boat and that forces us to haul in our fishing lines. When they leap out of the water, we can see their white undersides and their tail flukes as they once again disappear underwater. I watch in awe as these marine creatures breach around us and sometimes swim underneath our boat. Their presence ends our fishing for cod because we have to cease operations until the whales depart our area. Although they appear to be harmless, I would not like to fall overboard when they are around. In my imagination, I can picture myself riding on the back of a humpback, but I am soon brought back to reality.

While out fishing one day, we heard Albert exclaim, "See that one!"

We all looked to see where he was looking. One of the whales swam casually along by the port side of our boat and there was a smaller one that was apparently swimming closely with it. We surmised it must be a female with her offspring.

Pods of potheads or pilot whales as they are more commonly known, also disrupt our fishing at times throughout the season when they encounter and chase schools of capelin, squid, herring, or mackerel. The pods often range from six to twenty animals. They put on quite a show when encountering prey and grabbing mouthfuls as they move through the water; they sometimes toss their prey in the air. We can only watch in amazement as they gorge themselves and surface only to inhale more air for other attempts. It appears the whales disrupt the schools of capelin and mackerel whereby they become somewhat disoriented and more vulnerable to capture. The natural schooling phenomenon that provides safety in numbers for the fish appears to provide the whales with greater chance for success. Capelin, herring, mackerel, and squid are fish we use for bait and food. Therefore, we are in competition with whales and other marine creatures, but this kind of competition we don't mind.

Father told me that whales are hunted and killed and pothead whales in particular are very vulnerable because they travel in pods. By being together, it is easier to kill them. Sometimes they are even driven ashore by men in boats. Oddly enough too, potheads have been known to beach themselves for reasons unknown. I have tried to interpret father's words when we encounter potheads to try and make sense of it all. I can understand wanting to kill them to earn money, but doing it in such a dramatic way and killing so many leave some blanks in my understanding. Anyway, the potheads seem to be very resistant; we sight them every year while we are fishing and living here on the Island.

It is difficult for me to comprehend all that I see. I try to understand the interactions of the fish, whales, dolphins and birds in relation to our own fishing operations. We are trying to catch fish so that our family can continue to survive, while all sea creatures are also trying to survive. We are part of their way of life, and their existence is influenced by our activities. They compete with us in a way, but we bear no malice toward them. Fishing families on the Island have learned to exist with all marine creatures.

Even from the confines of the Island, we frequently see whales making their way through Conception Bay. It is while we are fishing that we get close up with them and have a chance to observe their actions. While I have heard many stories about whale activities, there has not been even one story involving negative encounters with them from a safety point of view. I suppose if we leave them alone, they have no reason to cause us any harm. Even though I have seen them many times, I always enjoy their presence, and it gives us a pleasant break in our fishing operations.

Although I miss some of my friends and the activities I enjoy back in town, the experiences enjoyed while fishing are those that many, many people may never experience. There are times when I consider myself lucky amid the hardships of living here on the Island.

CHAPTER SIX

Education

School doesn't have much importance for me during the fishing season. I am learning from my father and others by what we could classify as 'on-the-job' training or apprenticeship. I will gradually learn all there is to know of the practical aspects of fishing.

Yet, something is missing. Though I know how to perform certain tasks, I am not aware of the many reasons for doing them. When hauling in our boats, I know that if friction is reduced, the job becomes easier. Also, if a block and tackle is used, it makes many jobs much easier. Why is this so? Those types of answers can and must come from books and teachers. It is fun and rewarding to read books and have a better appreciation for the sea, the fish, the weather, people and places, and to be able to use that knowledge in daily life. Instead, my assistance is needed to help us all make a living and formal education is of lesser priority. It isn't that my parents have no respect for education, but other things come first in our scheme of things. Fishing is the generator that keeps our family going in every aspect of our lives and is our means of survival.

Therefore, my education is a mixture of formal study and practical training. Here on the Island, how well I can do tasks is more important than why I do them. I know a little about every aspect of fishing. However, this confined knowledge has the effect of keeping me further isolated from the world around me. I long for the opportunity to learn more and find out what other people are doing.

Our ritualistic move to the Island in May is accepted by our teachers. While they promote the importance of a formal education, they know the practicalities of our situation and are realistic in their understanding. There is certainly no animosity shown toward us, or negative repercussions, as we take our early departure from school in May. Since we don't get back from the Island until October, we are also late in starting the school term each year. Bringing school books or any formal school work to the Island is not an option, but some of us have a few books to read on our own as time and place permits. There is very little time for our parents to sit with us and ponder over books because fishing is a daylight-to-dark obligation. Beside, most parents have only the basic education when it comes to formal schooling, and education ranks second to making the fishing enterprise a success. However, as I participate in our family enterprise, there is always a profound interest in learning more about other people and places, and much of that requires reading about it.

Making up for lost time at school at the beginning of each school-year never presents a problem, and after a short while we are keeping pace with the rest of the class. Not that we are smarter than the rest of our schoolmates, but I believe we know that extra effort is required, and we just do what is necessary to make up for lost time. Teachers are very understanding and willing to give us extra attention to pick up the slack. They have pride in getting the most from students and helping us all to succeed. There is no doubt we have to undertake extra study and do more written work when we start school each fall to get to the level of the other students in our classes. After that, it is smooth sailing. It is common for teenagers to leave school altogether in grades nine to eleven and help support the family if required, by fishing or through some other occupation.

Here on the Island, I am becoming a 'fine young man' at least that is what the older folks say to me. I can row the boat, prong the fish, gut the fish, tend the gardens, chop wood, spread fish, carry water, and use a hammer to fix fences. Besides, I am learning how to act more mature and look after myself, well to a certain degree anyway.

It is interesting how the maturity of us boys sort of evolves from one fishing season to another. No one tells us we have now reached the age to perform a certain task. You perform it when you show that it is within your capability. The capacity to do work is not tied to age, but to physical and mental maturity. We are always given the opportunity to take on new tasks, and help is around when required if the task proves too great.

There is clearly a division of labour in regard to male and female. There are jobs for males and jobs for females. Yet there are shared jobs, such as spreading the fish, tending the gardens, and helping in the stages. Now washing clothes and preparing meals are not part of my vocabulary. No sir, no sissy jobs for me. Give me the more manly jobs like hauling nets and pronging fish where the sweat runs down your neck and callouses appear on your hands. Of course, I still have great respect for the type of work done by my sisters, just don't ask me to do any of it.

My sisters also learn many other types of practical duties from mother such as cooking, baking, sewing, knitting, making beds, helping on the flakes, and maintaining the shack. You could consider them the support group for our fishing operation. Without them life would be rather intolerable. I can't imagine cooking for myself and I certainly wouldn't want father to do it. It is therefore, a distinct advantage to have mother and the girls with us. The female side of our family has the ability to produce more comfort from the meagre circumstances of life on the Island and make our existence more enjoyable and tolerable. All the family work well together, but the bottom line is a good voyage. Indeed, every family on the Island works together, and sharing is commonplace because each fishing enterprise has the same objective.

Just like us boys, the girls are obliged to grow up rather quickly in this kind of environment. Somehow, mother has the knack of instilling in Bessie and Lill the feminine qualities as well as the practical and manual skills required for this Island way of life. Not much by some standards. Yet this is the life we all know.

In a somewhat strange way, we look forward to the Island fishery. For me it is as close to a vacation as I am going to get so I might as well make the best of it. The change in scenery each year gives me a different perspective, but each year indicates that the older I become the more responsibility and hardship I am to endure as part of our fishing enterprise. In that sense, I often imagine myself doing something else, as did many other of my friends on the Island. A few of us dream of moving away when older to a far-distant way of life while others talk about various vocations like teaching or owning a business. All that seems so far away from us now. What would the rest of my life be like?

Although we are confined to the Island, there is a realization that our abject existence has a certain sense of freedom. In the same way, while we work for the most part to make a living, on many occasions it is considered enjoyable and the rewards are shared by the whole family. Some of those so-called educated people can probably study this and write pages and pages about it. For us, it is simply a life with very little room for ego because the family works as a unit. What one person does is done for all. The bottom line is survival of the family, and how well we survive depends on the success of our fishing season each year. As one of my teachers said, "It is an artisanal, socioeconomic existence derived from the geography and nature of our location." That is not the way I would describe it, even though it may sound good to those with advanced learning.

The Bustle of Fishing

Life on the Island is more of a bustle since the cod struck in, and the results from the first landings of fish can be seen in the stages. The gardens here and in town show evidence of growing crops, and Molly is out to graze with the other horses. We don't have the horse to help us with the gardens here, so we do all the digging and planting. Concentration is centred on the fishing activity itself and that takes up all the time of the men and boys with the assistance of the women and girls.

Cod traps and hand-lines are reaping good catches and capelin are plentiful. This means long days for father and the older ones. Since everything is done manually, it takes considerable time to process the catch each day, especially when catches are exceptionally good. On some days trap crews are unable to handle all their catch and they share with those who are not so successful. It looks like it is going to be a good summer, or 'a good voyage,' as father calls it. In our stage the puncheons and pens of salted fish are becoming full and extra room will soon be required to permit more salting. It is time to start washing and drying the fish and that will provide space again.

Our salmon net has provided us with a few salmon. Atlantic salmon are really beautiful and very tasty, too. One of the biggest salmon we caught was estimated to weigh fifteen pounds. I felt proud that day as I stepped ashore holding the big salmon with the bright silvery scales sparkling in the sun. This one was not salted, but cut up and boiled with salt pork as a special treat. I don't know of anything that can beat the taste of fresh salmon and potatoes all boiled together with perfection, in the same pot.

Bob and I have managed to secure a few barrels of capelin that we salted. We place them on 'skivers' and hang them up to dry on the outside of the stage. The flies find them and congregate in large numbers during the first few hours. However, the drying process soon eliminates most of the moisture in them and the flies are no longer present. The salted capelin will be placed in brin/burlap bags and used as food during the winter. We have to be careful not to let them get too dry, or father will not be exceedingly happy. When they are too dry he refers to eating them as like eating sticks.

A few of the smaller boys like Walt take some of the capelin and split them like we do with the cod. They pretend they are fishermen and imitate the process we are doing. It has become a great pastime, and it is fun watching them spreading out the capelin to dry, knowing full well I probably did the same thing when I was their age. At least it keeps them busy for a few hours each day. However, I have no more time to watch them now.

Every able-bodied person is pressed into service. Most mornings, I experience daybreak in the boat while tending the hand-lines, and each nightfall we put the final touches to our day's catch. We are fortunate to have a large family because it means more people to participate in chores.

Religion

All families on the Island are Church of England. Thus there is one less thing to fight about. Although we do not have regular church services, there is a respect for doctrine and we still maintain our religious habits. The Bible's teaching of working for six days and resting on the seventh is practised, but no extra effort is made to travel to town and attend church.

No fishing activity is carried out on Sunday which is considered the day of rest. It is sort of a fun day for youngsters and a time to reflect on the previous week's activities without the rigours of work. Frustration, pressure, and stress are not evident on that day, except for mother and the girls who have to cook, since apparently everybody still wants to eat on Sunday, me included.

The highlight of Sunday for us is the appearance of Mr. Austin Snow's daughter, Emmie Snow, who holds Sunday School without fail. She gathers us all in her father's fish stage and relates Bible stories and then questions us about the story. On fine sunny Sundays, we all gather outside the stage on the grass. She has taught herself to play the accordion and plays very well but certainly not as good as some members of the Frenches' households. A couple of them can make the accordion talk.

Most of all, we love to sing the hymns as she plays the accordion. She is the kind of lively person who can put some enjoyment even into prayers and hymns, making the whole process more exciting for us. It's regarded as an opportunity for children to get together and it keeps our previous religious teachings intact.

On one late July Sunday we receive a visit from Reverend W.R.J. Higgitt, minister of St. Paul's Church, our regular place of worship in Harbour Grace. St. Paul's was built in 1835 and is the oldest stone church in the Dominion of Newfoundland. We never know when Rev. Higgitt is going to visit and each time he arrives it is a surprise. The service is held outside where everyone just sits around on the grass in casual fashion as prayers and hymns are said and sung. What a time it is, Reverend Higgitt trying to say prayers, and the animals nonchalantly wandering among the people with the gulls flying overhead. God must be laughing to himself. Today we all sing a very appropriate hymn as the dogs, cats, goats, and gulls sometimes chime in:

All things bright and beautiful
All creatures great and small
All things wise and wonderful
The Lord God made them all

As a matter of fact, I would rather listen to the goats singing than some of the women. The goats have longer necks, which probably allows them to reach the high notes more easily. Yes, we have a mixture of singers all right. There are those who can sing, those who think they can, those who wished they could, and the rest just sing anyway. However, if God can put up with it, I suppose I can too.

It is on this occasion mother catches me impersonating Mrs. Noel, John Noel's wife, as she sings, and I am at the time, getting a few laughs from friends around me. I detected a slight smile from mother, but from her other expressions I can tell that my impersonations should be stopped immediately. I know what she is demanding even though she says nothing.

Reverend Higgitt usually visits two or three times during the summer to hold a service and meet with his Island flock. It certainly takes the routineness out of his work and he appears to enjoy each outing. He also receives an amount of dried fish to take back with him.

The Sunday School in town holds an annual summer picnic each year, but of course we do not attend. However, they always send some picnic goodies to us children on the Island.

The Animals

I find it difficult to distinguish pets and food in regard to our Island animals. The goats, Rosie and Daisy, are an integral part of the family. They come when you call their names whether it is milking time or feeding time. They are a source of milk, but pets at the same time.

Sport our setter is a pet, but also a hunting dog for partridge. We have a special small sled for him and he is a good help in hauling firewood out from the forest in the winter. He displays somewhat more intelligence than the goats and can do a number of simple actions on command. One of my favourites that show his ability has to do with father.

It's customary on Sunday afternoons for father and a bunch of the other men to get together at the far end of the Island. There they will look out to sea, smoke their pipes, and spin a few yarns in relative peace and quiet. When supper is ready mother says to Sport, "Go get father."

Sport runs to the end of the Island, locates father, and then barks a couple of times before starting to head back to the shack. When he is sure father is on his way, he keeps going. If father doesn't move, he continues to bark. Of course Sport knows he will get his supper, too.

I found a young gull and turned it into a pet for the summer. It's not easy to change a wild bird into a domesticated chick in such a short period. The gull can't fly away because I have clipped its wings. Without the wing feathers flight is impossible, and the bird just wanders around its enclosure and is very tame with me. I suppose the isolationism of the Island helps to wean the chick from its natural surroundings. I spend considerable time studying its movements and beside, it is a hit with my friends. After a few weeks, Pawk as I have called him, begins to eat regularly and is not disturbed as much by the sights and sounds around him. His name comes from the sort of sound he makes, especially when frightened. There are times when I look at him in confinement with the gulls flying overhead, and think that perhaps he should be allowed to fly freely with them. However, in the final analysis, I consider that the natural tendency to fly will be offset somewhat by the fact that food is brought to him and he doesn't have to hunt for it. More time will elapse before Pawk and I part company, and even Sport learns to live with him.

Young gulls are easy to catch if you can locate them soon after they are hatched and still unable to fly. When approached, they have a natural tendency to hide down among the rocks that very closely resemble their mottled colours, and stick their heads underneath their bodies in a complete camouflage. Unless you are watching closely, they look like the rocks and are difficult to discern. They lie still without any movement whatsoever, obscure in their surroundings just as nature intended. You can even touch them and they will not move. Therefore, they are easy to pick up once you spot them. This ability to lie still even in a time of fear is the only defence they have. When they get a little older, their legs and feet can propel them through the water if they want to escape from land. Then gradually they learn to fly and that is ultimate freedom.

I'm not sure what the gulls think of our taking over their territory for about six months each year. It is sort of a mutual arrangement, because in return for the land, we provide them with food in the form of fish waste. It can't be too bad for them as we are still here and they continue to flourish.

One of the other boys told me that in past years a few residents would build pens for the young gulls they caught and then feed them fish scraps until they matured. The gulls would then be killed and used for making soup, gull soup *du jour*. But not for me. I can't visualize Pawk as soup material. Every advantage is taken to provide food and the presence of gulls is no exception for some people.

One marine bird of particular interest for food is the locally called turr, but known generally as murre. Why these birds were given the local name I don't know and have never heard anyone explain. Sometimes these birds will show up late in the fishing season, and a shotgun is always in the boat just in case we happen to encounter any of them. They most often travel in small flocks. In the hopes of bagging a few, we often take trips to specific areas around the Island where we know turrs are sometimes found.

I was out in the boat on one of those hunting trips late in the season with Bill and Albert last year. We had spotted a few turrs while fishing the previous day, so my brothers figured our hunting chances on this day would be good. We did locate a few birds and Bill was the one handling the shotgun. He fired first at a few birds while they were in the water and later fired at another two birds in flight but with no success. Albert was becoming a bit concerned about the ability of Bill after the two missed shots and suggested to him that he couldn't hit the side of a barn. Bill was little upset with his remark and retorted, "I did come close. Didn't you see the feathers fly off that turr after my last shot?"

Then Albert, in a rather dramatic tone, responded, "You shoot them first, and we can pick the feathers from them afterwards."

Before we headed for home, Bill had managed to bag six turrs. Hunting with my older brothers is usually good fun and always a few laughs. Also, I know what kind of meat stew we would have the next day. Some people don't like the somewhat oily taste of marine birds, but that doesn't apply to our family.

It was during hunting trips like this that I learned more about using a shotgun. No matter who I was with, they would often let me fire a few shots, but only when they had already shot a few birds. Every one of my misses was a laugh for them. Standing in a moving boat makes the target more difficult to hit, and it takes a while to figure it all out. I get to be a little better each time, but this learning experience, as with others, is gained from trial and error. How many more errors do I have to make?

CHAPTER SEVEN

Fishing Continues

July is a good fishing month, and the flakes are covered with fish each day to take advantage of the sunny drying weather. Women are busy on the flakes, spreading the fish in the morning and turning it again in the afternoon. If the day is too hot and without any wind, they have to ensure the fish do not become sunburnt. The fastest time they work is when a sudden shower of rain forces them to gather all the fish and place it under cover. This is a time when everybody helps unless we are out on the fishing grounds.

Weather is the most important element to our success apart from the availability of fish. If the weather and sea conditions are bad, we are prevented from using our boats to go fishing. Even a strong undertow with little wind is enough to reduce our catches. Unless we have sunny weather, we are not able to dry our fish. Weather rules our lives and our economy and we live with nature every day by learning how to deal with all its adversities. Rain and light wind does not stop fishing operations, but really slows down the drying process.

As a matter of fact, we often obtain good catches when the wind is moderate and rain is falling. I have mentioned that fact to father, but he did not seem to have much of an explanation. He did say that the sea conditions might appear darker during cloudy and rainy periods which could induce cod to move more in search of food. Also, the bait on our lines may be more visible to the fish in the darker water. I don't know if he was serious or if he made that response up at the spur of the moment just to give me an answer.

Bill, Albert, George, and Bob handle most of the harder work with father. I am just old enough to really be of help in most of the minor jobs and a certain number of the major activities. Brother Walt is only six and too young for the heavy tasks. Mother has him helping her when she is in the stage just to have him near so she can watch him. If the stage area is really busy, she leaves him with Bessie, who along with Lill, ensures his safety. Mothers who have smaller youngsters often tie them with rope to the stages while they are working so they will not fall overboard. This is just a slight change from the normal. Instead of tying up the dogs and letting the youngsters run free, the youngsters are tied up and the dogs run free. Parents have found out that accidents can happen quickly to their children when they are busily engaged in and around any activity on the Island. The sea is never very far away.

While mother is busy in the stage, my sisters often take care of the cooking and the washing. We have an eaves-trough on one side of the sloping shack roof that catches the rainwater and directs it into a barrel. This provides the water used for washing. Someone also has to bring water from the well, using the buckets and hoop. That wooden hoop was somebody's brainstorm. How easy it makes the carrying of water. Someone must have been carrying buckets of water and found out it was difficult because the buckets keep hitting your legs. They must have asked themselves the question, "What can I do to keep that from happening? It has to be something that is not too heavy but wide enough to keep the buckets away from the body uniformly on each side. What about if I tried a round hoop from an apple or a fish barrel?" Thus a hoop became popular and it is a thoughtful invention that serves us well.

I'm not sure the girls think the washboard is such a good invention. That thing must be hard on the knuckles trying to scrub clothes across it. After an hour of using that contraption you must feel like throwing it over the cliff. Anyway, the clothes hanging on the clothesline look nice and clean, and I have no complaints about the cleanliness of my apparel.

On one particular, beautiful late July morning, I breathe in the wholesome, warm, salty air as we drift over the calm water. We just finished hand-lining and have about five or six quintals of fish. We've been out here since 4:30 a.m., and the morning sunrise is blinding as it appears to lift out of the sea, sending bright rays across the water. The dawning of another day in Conception Bay. The codfish in the boat signifies plenty of work ahead. There is a measure of pride, however, in knowing the sea has been good to us today by providing a bountiful catch.

Whales can be seen breaking the surface of the water as they come up for air and begin another descent into the depths. Father points out the different kinds of whales as we get to know most of them from their fins and their tail actions. The humpbacks are delightful to watch as they surface and then seem to wave their tail flukes before completely disappearing again. Porpoises pass along our stern and disappear out into the Bay.

Gannets are fun to watch too, as they dive from the sky to strike their underwater prey. How streamlined they look plummeting from the sky in deadly pursuit, neck stretched out and wings tucked away, striking the water with what can be described as a knife-cutting motion. Slowly they surface with a fish in their beak, signifying a successful dive.

Finally, father says the words I have been waiting for all morning: "It's boil-up time," as he reaches for the caboose.

This item has nothing to do with a train, but is an old iron pot used as a stove on board the boat. The splits are put in the caboose and the fire lit before laying on the kettle. Very soon we have a mug of strong tea, sweetened with sugar and diluted with fresh goat's milk. I'm not sure if it was Rosie's or Daisy's, but it didn't make any difference. Mother's homemade bread sure tastes good now that the molasses spread on it earlier has managed to soak right through. Nothing like a big mug of strong tea and molasses bread out on the water when you are good and hungry. Ah, this is the life.

We head for the stage at around eleven a.m. with our load of fish, and mother is there to greet us. She is anxious for our return because today we have to make a trip to Harbour Grace to take care of some chores there. Quickly we prong the fish from the boat and get the splitting and salting operations underway. The women have already spread the salted fish on the flakes and the rest of the day should be good for drying.

Mother is insisting that we all have dinner before father takes her, Walt, and me to town. No need to ask what we are having for dinner because today is Monday and we always have leftovers from Sunday's dinner.

Dinner is the midday meal for us which fits our fishing activities. Since father and the older boys, including me most times, are up early and usually not finished with the fish until around midday, this is the best time to have the family meal and is the only fully cooked meal for the day. At about three in the afternoon they are out in the boat again and may not finish in the stage until after dark. This fishing life means not much sleep and irregular meals. Considering the work of father and the older boys, it is easy to see how important the participation of the women is in the whole scheme of things to keep our fishing enterprise working smoothly.

I'm looking forward to this trip to Harbour Grace that will last for about six days, depending on weather. Very soon the four of us are on our way. There is a slight breeze from the southwest as I help father with the rowing. In just over two hours later, we arrive. Father takes just enough time to look around at the house and gardens before heading for the boat again and the return trip to the Island. Bess and Lill have remained on the Island and will care for father and the rest of the boys while mother is in town. The care of the shack, cooking, washing, plus other chores are all left in their hands.

Mother takes me aside and relates to me the jobs that we have to do while in town. The main job is to make the rest of the hay and that entails spreading it each day for the sun to dry. Mother has a few jobs to do around the house, but it is really a holiday for her too, when compared to life on the Island. Here in town we have the house and all the comforts of home.

One job for me is to whitewash the fences around the house. It is imperative to have our property well maintained. Whitewash is nothing more than lime mixed with water, but it sure makes the fences look white. Walt can even help me as long as he gets more lime on the fence than he does on himself. Looking at him as we whitewash the fence, I'm not sure he did.

This break in routine gives me the opportunity to spend some time with my friends and to play games, too. However, I have to ensure that my work is done before father comes back or things may really get exciting for me. Mother makes sure I am kept on track each day and before we know it, father arrives back for us. He is glad to see we have the hay all dried and in pooks, and the fences looking sparkling white.

However, father's mind is preoccupied with the Island, and after what seemed the briefest of pauses, we are in the boat and making our way eastward. The day is pleasant and serene as we row past the lighthouse on Point of Beach with father telling us about the past few days of fishing. The weather has not been too bad for fishing, but there was not ample wind to help dry the fish as he would have liked. Before long, sights on the Island come more into view and we look astern at Salvage Rock as it fades more and more into the distance.

Bess and Lill are the first to greet us as we hit shore, probably glad that mother is once again on the scene and in charge. Walt and I quickly disappear and are most anxious to tell of our exploits in town to our Island friends. This jubilancy for me is short lived and before long I am again involved in 'yaffling' the fish off the flakes and helping to secure it for the night. Besides, I am eager because I know next Wednesday is my one big annual trip to the Regatta at Lady Lake.

Regatta Day

I am really looking forward to Regatta Day and my first-time chance to participate in the rowing races on Lady Lake plus partaking in the festivities at lakeside. It is a town holiday and many residents gather at lakeside to spend the day with family, friends, and visitors. A large number bring prepared food or food items to cook over an open fire. Men place bets on individual races, not to make money, but to make the experience a little more meaningful. The boat races bring much excitement for all those gathered for this annual event. The anticipation mounts when the blast from the shotgun and accompanying music signal the start of each race. Then all eyes are on the boats as they make their way up the lake, before turning the buoys and heading down again, where a shotgun blast signals the crossing of the finish line by each boat. The end of each race always means joy for some and disappointment for others. Each winning crew will have bragging rights until the next year.

Although it is a big holiday for most town people, my family stays on the Island. However, father makes no fuss whatsoever about my taking the day off to enjoy it. One of my buddies here on the Island, Ron Ash, will be joining me. Ron is the best buddy I have on the Island and every spare minute we have, and those are few, we can usually find something different to occupy our interests. We spend more time together when living in town.

Finally it is Regatta Day, the last Wednesday of July, and the morning is beautiful with only a very light breeze. I could hardly sleep in anticipation of the day. Mother makes sure I have a good breakfast and packs a snack of molasses cookies for the trip.

While in town a few weeks previously, Ron and I came up with a plan that would give us some cash to use on Regatta Day. We enticed one of our neighbours in Harbour Grace to buy a ten-pound tub of salted fish sounds that we had cut from cod and stored in Ron's fathers stage. He would pay us ninety cents for them. "Do you have the tub of sounds," I bellowed to Ron as he made his way toward the boat.

"Indeed I do," he called back.

We put our tub of fish sounds aboard the boat and soon we are underway. There is a feeling of enthusiasm as we leave the Island, soaking up the sunshine and gradually putting the town closer and closer. There is no requirement for us to practise our rowing skills because we have to row every day, except Sunday, while fishing. In fact, we are rowing over three miles now just to reach the wharf in Harbour Grace.

Ron, like myself is small and wiry with not an ounce of fat. The only thing covering our bones is muscle although they don't bulge like those of my older brothers. We consider ourselves in good shape from rowing and playing soccer. Our skill in handling boats should be some advantage in our race today. However, winning was not our prime consideration. It was the chance to participate that excited us more.

This is the sixtieth year of the Regatta at Lady Lake. The first one was sponsored by the Harbour Grace Volunteer Fire Company in July 1862. Actually, the first recorded race took place at Harbour Grace Harbour in 1859 between two crews entered by a Captain Walsh and a Mr. Edward Oke. It was a three-mile course from Point of Beach in the east to Long Beach in the west and return. The winner was Mr. Oke, who coxswained his own crew of William C. Snow, William J. Snow, Thomas Snow, and Charles Ash. The prize, $25, was shared among all crew members.

This piece of history gives Ron and me more incentive to display our rowing skills because we have a family name and reputation to uphold.

Finally, we reach our destination and the first thing to do was deliver the fish sounds. We took care of that chore in haste. "Here's your forty-five cents," said Ron as he counted out the money.

It is still about a two-mile walk to Lady Lake, but we make the journey in a short time, running much of the way. Crowds of people are there and we can see that many families have a fire going and eating dinner or at least a big lunch. Most people refer to it as a 'boil-up.' The Union Jacks are flying on the boathouse and at a number of locations along lakeside as people cheer on the crews in the first races of the day

Men can be seen betting on individual crews. Cheers are heard when a favourite crew reaches the finish line and the gun sounds. Excitement fills the air as the results of the bets are distributed to the winners.

Finally our race is called and Ron and I head for the wharf to board the whaler. We find our other two crew members, Fred and Norm, and now we are ready to row in the juvenile race.

Time to put our rowing skills to the test. One of the main considerations when rowing is to ensure that all crew members are in unison with the stroke-oarsman. Ron sits next to Fred, the stroke-oarsman and I am the forward man in the boat with Norm in between.

Although we are very adept at rowing alone, rowing as a team of four requires concentration and skill to maintain uniformity and ultimate good momentum. Each stroke of the oar will have me bending forward and then exerting pressure with my arms to allow my body to straighten again. Our coxswain provides us with a few parting words as we prepare to leave the boat dock.

The other three whalers along with ours head for the starting line and the coxswains finally jockey the boats into position to begin the race. Then at the sound of the starting gun, we are off and the music blares out as we head up the lake. The oars hit the water in fine fashion as we keep pace with our stroke-oarsman. About one-third through the race the four boats are not too far apart and neither seems to have much more than half a boat-length advantage at any one time. A close race it is. I try not to look at the other boats as we make our way up the lake, but a casual glance shows we may be ahead at this stage. Now and then coxswains can be heard edging their charges on, and our cox is no different. It looks like we are indeed in the lead but I am beginning to feel the effects of muscle exertion already. Other crewmembers must be feeling the same thing.

We enter the turn at the halfway-buoy to begin our final lap down the lake to the finish line. Turning the buoy takes a little toll on us because our oars for a short period were out of sync. We lose some ground to two of the other boats, and they complete their turn of the buoy in the lead. With our cox yelling, "Come on boys, give it all you got. Buckle those oars and make sure you maintain the stroke. Come on, come on, all you've got."

We have to make a big push to overtake those other two boats if we are to win the race. I expect that those two crews are similarly not thinking of letting us beat them. Turning the buoys is always a tricky part of each race and when not done successfully it can mean much lost time.

I pull on the oar with all I can muster, and the rest of the crew are doing the same as we attempt to put on a strong finish. About halfway down the lake I catch sight of the boat that now looks like it is in second position. Very soon it appears we have overtaken that boat, but I don't want to spend too much time looking except to ensure I maintain the pace of Fred, our stroke- oarsman.

We continue rowing, giving everything we got, on the final burst to the finish line in hopes of overtaking the lead boat. Nobody in our crew is looking now as we move along with our cox spurring us on as he keeps shouting "We're gaining, we're gaining," and I look forward to overtaking the lead boat and a resounding victory for us.

Very soon, I hear the repeat of the shotgun. The first boat has crossed the finish line, but it isn't us. I can also hear the shouts from the crowd. Within a few seconds another shotgun blast signifies our crossing, less than a half boat-length behind. Good, but not quite good enough.

Ron and I embrace Fred and Norm and congratulate each other on the race. I feel a certain sense of accomplishment as we pull our sweating bodies out of the boat to the well wishes of the crowd. We all enter the boathouse and give our best wishes to the winning crew and receive a bottle of soda pop for our effort. We don't consider the reward very important, nor is losing a major disappointment. The fun of participating and being in the spotlight is enough for my pride. Fred appears to take it a little more seriously, but gradually contents himself and says, "Oh well, we always have next year to try again," and we all agree.

Anyway, we did make the finish of the race very exciting for the spectators. However, amidst all the glamour associated with rowing, there is a slight sense of longing when Ron and I realize that another year will pass before having the chance to row again competitively.

We leave the boathouse and begin speaking with a number of our friends and a few adults who had watched the race. I pity those who had bet on us to win, but the comments coming our way are always in jest. One gentleman shouted to us as we passed, "I had my money on you and you rowed a good race. Better luck next year."

Hunger is on my mind and in my stomach as we seek out the best food value for the money we have. Ron and I spend some time with friends watching the other races as I swallow down a few morsels of food. Sometimes the races become so exciting that people wade out into the lake to try and see which boat is in the lead, and we are not immune to doing that either. After the conclusion of the championship race at the end the day, Ron and I have to think about our trip back to the Island. It may take us longer to walk to our boat and row back because our endurance has already been tested and we are somewhat tired. Father asked me to take a quick look around our house, and I did; Ron did the same at his house.

The trip back is indeed tiresome, due to our earlier rowing effort, and we are glad the wind has died out completely, as it often does in the evening. At least it is not foggy. We take turns rowing and reminiscing about today's trip and particularly about our race as we move steadily along. After what feels like a long time we are abreast of the Island.

We are sort of heroes as we make our way into the Launch Way and secure the boat. Ron's father and mine, along with a few others, are there to greet us as we answer questions about the various races held during the day, including our own. Of course, since nobody else witnessed the event, we are free to exaggerate at least a little bit. Ron was asked most of the questions because some of his cousins and uncles were crew members in other races. After providing enough information, Ron and his father finally head home to their own shack near Sandy Cove as darkness approaches.

Mother has a mug-up waiting for me as I enter the shack and is glad we have arrived back safely. She wants to know how I made out in the Regatta and I relate all my experience to her as a few remaining family members listen. She was also interested in the other races, but only in a very casual way. Following a short period of conversation with the rest of the family, I resign myself to sleep as the smell of father's pipe tobacco wafts throughout the shack. Bessie and Lill had no interest in my Regatta experience and were already settled for the night.

A Scary Event

The Island offers many places for potential accidents, but most residents undertake their daily tasks with caution and very few mishaps occur even though our surroundings include many cliffs and water is all around us. Parents are continually warning younger ones about particular areas to avoid, but that sometimes only piques their curiosity. Luckily, someone always seems to be watching to prevent any real harm, except for one occasion that ended up involving me.

Walt and his friend Eli, who was about the same age, had walked the path out past Eli's house on the eastern end of the Island toward Lobster Cove, sometimes called Lobster Gulch. Mother and the girls had been busy at their chores until Bessie suddenly realized that Walt was missing. The first place they began looking was the stage, but he was nowhere in sight. As the alarm about Walt's whereabouts spread, Mrs. Martin realized that Eli was also missing. Soon mother and others were searching different places, such as around stages and under flakes, when one of the Noseworthy children said she had seen both of them going out the path earlier in the morning. This prompted mother, Mrs. Martin, and a number of family members to run out the path shouting out their names as they covered all parts of the local area. Then it became evident that if they came this way and were nowhere in sight, the cliffs had to be involved. They continued to search along the edge of the cliffs when one of the women said she thought she heard a voice. They all stood still and sure enough, they heard two voices in the vicinity of Lobster Gulch so they hurried to the area. Although they could hear them, the boys were not easy to see from their first vantage point. However, mother, Bessie, and Lill moved around the Gulch to the other side, where they could see them in plain sight. Considering they were on a small ledge about twenty-five feet down, mother did not want to excite them too much because they might fall in the water so she tried to talk to them in a calming manner. They appeared to be all right, but were frightened and afraid to move.

Mother said, "I wonder how they got themselves down there without falling? They must have edged themselves down the embankment in the Gulch until they reached the small ledge and were too scared to attempt the climb back up again."

The climb up probably looked far worse to them than the climb down. In their position on the ledge, the face of the cliff must have looked really steep and the water below pounding into the Gulch looked treacherous. They were frozen in their positions without really appreciating the potential dangers.

Mother and Mrs. Martin continued saying things that hopefully would keep the boys calm until they could decide how to get them back up. None of the women wanted to take the chance on climbing down and even if they did, how would Walt and Eli climb up in their frightened condition? All the men and older boys were out fishing today and only the women and smaller children were left on the Island. What could they do?

While all this was happening, we arrived back from fishing and immediately knew that something was amiss because nobody was at the stage to meet us as usual. As soon as we began walking toward our shack, we could hear the commotion at the end of the Island. Finding nobody at home, we struck out immediately and were soon met by mother and the others. Mother explained the situation regarding Walt and Eli to father, who acted immediately. Hurriedly, he instructed, "Bill, you and Albert run and get two coils of rope from the stage."

All the while, mother and Mrs. Martin quietly resumed talking to Walt and Eli so that they would not become excited and fall from their perch. Calming words were given and the assurance that they would soon be rescued.

While father was waiting for the ropes, he pondered that if he dropped the ropes to the boys, they might be too young to secure themselves properly, or worst of all, may fall on the way up if the ropes slipped in their hands. Also, if someone were to climb down, there is a chance rocks could fall down on the boys. If an older person were let down on a rope, it would be difficult to pull him back up. Then he looked at me and said, "We will lower you down first. Then we will lower down another rope and you can secure each of them in turn before we start hauling them up. When Walt and Eli are safe, we will haul you up again."

Father said, "Tell them to spread their legs and keep their feet against the cliff on the way up because that would prevent them from injury and make it easier to haul them up over the side of the Gulch. We will haul them very slowly."

Soon the ropes arrived. He tied a bowline knot in one end of each of the two ropes and then passed the other end through the loop that would securely fasten us in the rope. I seated myself in one of the ropes and turning my back to the water, proceeded to let myself be lowered slowly down to the ledge and the boys. In order to prevent rocks or other debris from falling down on the boys, they told me I would be lowered down about ten feet away and then guided over to where the boys were. Father, George, and Albert manned the rope and I kept my feet toward the cliff to allow the rope to slide down easily until I was standing next to the boys. They were glad to see me and gave me awkward smiles of relief. Mother's shout from the other side of the Gulch let everyone know that I had reached the ledge. Now they lowered another rope that I caught and started to make ready for Eli.

I quickly but cautiously told him, "Fasten the rope around you like you are sitting in a swing, hang onto the rope with both hands, and keep your legs apart and feet toward the cliff during the climb so you can sort of bounce your way up."

He looked a little scared at first, but finally indicated he was ready. "All ready," I shouted over to mother.

She quickly let father and the others know they could begin hauling. After what seemed like a long time, Eli was safe at the top, much to Mrs. Martin's relief as she hurried over to him.

As soon as Eli was released they sent the rope down again and I gave Walt the same instructions. No need for too much explanation this time. He was probably more scared of reaching the top and meeting father than he was for the actual climb up the cliff. Mother shouted to me to be sure he was fastened in the rope properly. Then mother echoed my word that all was ready to begin hauling Walt to the top. Her last instruction was, "My God Tom, be really careful hauling him up."

Walt gave me a quick last glance as he began moving up the cliff and maintaining his footing to keep away from the side. Then he was finally out of my sight and presumably safe at the top.

Now it was my turn to leave the ledge, and since I already had a rope around me, all they had to do was begin hauling. Mother was watching and she shouted to me, "Are you ready?"

"I'm ready," was my quick reply and I heard her indicating to father and the others to begin hauling as she too, ran over to where father and all the others were located.

Very soon, I was face-to-face with father and George as they hauled me over the edge to safety and to the relief of all. The rescue was over. It is an ordeal that both Eli and Walt will never forget and was a lesson for the younger ones. Mother and Mrs. Martin were especially relieved and showed it.

Eli and Walt told their story about how they happened to end up down in Lobster Gulch. They had actually planned to climb down to the water's edge. The climb down was not too difficult as they lowered themselves on the protruding rocks sticking out on the side of the Gulch, but when they reached the ledge and looked up, it appeared so much steeper and they became scared. Looking down at the sea washing into the Gulch was not very reassuring either. Now they were stuck without knowing what to do. It was probably a good thing they did not try climbing back up again because one slip and it would all be over.

Lobster Gulch is a somewhat feared place on the Island because a number of years ago a gentleman lost his life after falling off the cliff there. The gentleman was a great-uncle of mine, and it is still a mystery as to how it happened.

CHAPTER EIGHT

Selling Our Fish

Father has a business relationship with the merchant company W.J. Moores, in Carbonear. It is a shared-risk venture, whereby the merchant provides supplies and provisions in return for our fish. At the end of the fishing season when all fish are sold, a settlement is made, or as Father likes to call it, a reconciliation. This means that the costs of supplies and provisions are deducted from the proceeds of the fish sales and father receives the balance, if there is one. I have also heard the day of reconciliation called the day of reckoning. If the voyage is good, both father and the firm gain. If the voyage is poor, then the merchant probably has to extend credit, and we have to do without certain things. In some respects, the merchant is gambling because he advances credit to father early in the year in the hope that receivables in the form of fish will be available later as payment.

This sort of paternalistic arrangement ties father to the company, but although the arrangement is not great, it is satisfactory. Of course, as long as we are landing good catches, the merchant's risk is eliminated.

Today we are preparing for our first delivery of sun-dried, heavy salted fish to Carbonear. We have about twelve quintals ready for sale. Father does his own final inspection and is pleased with this first load. Good-quality fish will give father an advantage in negotiating with the company. As father says, "The less ammunition we can give the company to justify lowering the price, the better it will be for his negotiating position."

Bill and I load the last of the dried fish and we soon set sail for Carbonear. Passing Bristol's Hope, we are heading toward the wharf of W.J. Moores on the north side of the harbour. Father takes part in the usual exchange of pleasantries with company workers while we prepare to unload. The company's cullers sort our fish according to grade and place them in separate piles. Father intently watches and sometimes questions the decision of a culler. After all, it is their decisions that determine the amount of money we will receive. Father knows it is not prudent to upset the cullers because then they might grade the fish harder. Therefore, he has to draw a fine line between pushing for our rights while at the same time maintaining good relationships. He seems to know what he is doing in that regard.

Mr. Moores is anxious to find out what kind of a voyage we are having in order to anticipate future sales. Father and he talk generally about the fish we have just landed and Bill and I stand around and listen without entering into the conversation. Very soon it is time to get a receipt for our sales and he tells father to go over and see Si, his son who also works for the company. This receipt is one of a number father will use to calculate final settlement in the fall.

On the way back Bill mentions that he thought a few of the fish could have received a higher grade. However, father figures we have done very well. There appears to be a mutual respect between Mr. Moores and father, even though there may have been times of disagreement. You win some and you lose some. Anyway, this co-adventurer type of arrangement is not conducive to becoming rich, regardless of catches, and father has no visions of grandeur. He is satisfied with what he has accomplished today.

I have listened to father and other fishermen discuss the business of dealing with merchants, and even with my limited knowledge and understanding, I can see that the system in which we operate tends to favour the merchants. Operating a fishing enterprise like ours is very risky because as each year begins we don't really know how much fish we will catch. It is speculative risk. Even when we do have a good voyage, prices often drop. Father has tried to explain to me how merchants tend to lower fish prices if we have more fish to sell. That is why merchants are always anxious to find out early if we are having a good year. It is also the reason father tends to sell only a small lot of fish on our first visit to the merchant. He wants to test the market to give him an idea of how much he can expect. If the merchant finds out we have had a good year, he may reduce the initial prices. Father knows too that if he negotiates a good price, the merchant can try to reduce the amount paid by lowering the fish grades because each grade of fish is paid a different price. The higher the grade, the higher the price.

It is not easy for father to gain any advantage over the merchant, but he has a very good reputation with Mr. Moores. Father frequently has differences of opinion with him about quality, and dialogue between the two can sometimes get nasty, but it is interspersed with banter that finally leads to a settlement. Father refers to it as 'give and take.' But no matter how the negotiations go, there is always the feeling that the merchant does most of the taking.

However, father explains that he can push the merchant only so far in negotiations, and arguments have to be tempered with the pricing information put forward by the merchant. You really can't afford to offend the merchant because in the following spring it may be necessary to ask for credit to purchase fishing supplies. After a few years of dealing with the same merchant, father has maintained a good working relationship, and is satisfied with the quality and prices received for the most part. However, he would like to get more.

I try to listen as much as I can when father is dealing with him so that I can learn from their actions. Father, with limited education, says that Mr. Moores often talks about the supply and demand for fish. It is difficult for me to justify in my own mind why the price goes down for us when we have a good supply and also goes down for us when the demand goes down. We lose when the supply is good and when the demand is poor. Good or bad, we lose. I suppose I will understand this process in another few years.

Contentment

August is the month that brings a sigh of relief and a state of contentment to us on the Island. Every fishing crew this year has enjoyed a very good harvest of fish to date, even as the fishing and fish-drying continues. There is some relief in knowing that this voyage will at least provide ample amounts of fish to sell to get us through another winter. The good harvest of fish also means more activity and promotes a better feeling among the families. The success of the harvest brings success for the whole Island population. There is a sense of happiness as each family participates in the day-to-day operation of their fishing enterprises. It is expressed in conversation and even the youngsters know that this year is a very good one. The mood of the Island is upbeat, brought about by the full flakes of fish drying in the sun.

Being on an island and relatively isolated, we are I suppose somewhat of an attraction. Although we probably don't think so, it must look different for anyone visiting to see families living in shacks with very little in the way of conveniences or amenities. While our purpose for being here is well established, to some visitors who do not understand the fishing mentality, we may appear strange indeed.

Many people in Harbour Grace visit friends and relatives on the Island on Sundays. On this one occasion they came in Mr. Ern Sheppard's big, open boat that is thirty feet long and capable of carrying a large number of people. He often did of his own free will, ferry visitors to and from the Island at no cost to them. While on the Island, many visitors spend time in the shacks having a cup of tea and some chit-chat. It is an opportunity to catch up on the news in town and often get a few favours done. Our family looks forward to those visits as do other families, because it breaks up the monotony of life here. While it might be a novelty for visitors, it serves as an outlet for us to find out new things and talk about other subjects to take us away from our routine way of life, even if only for one day. It often gives the visitors a chance to see our life in action and revive old acquaintances. For some it means a meal of newly-dried salt fish, too.

As this Sunday afternoon comes to an end and the last of our visitors step aboard Mr. Sheppard's boat, there is a wave of goodbyes all around. Sport and I watch the boat head out of sight around the Island until it disappears. He turns and licks my hand to remind me I still have a friend, even though the others have gone. I accept his friendship as we race to the shack for supper.

The next day when we arrive from the fishing grounds, there is another group of visitors who have come to have a look at us. These are more sophisticated, most obvious by their apparel. Tourists I suppose you would call them. They turn out to be the Tapp family who are visiting home from the United States. Although they speak more eloquently and sport fine clothes, they still know a capelin when they see one.

They are anxious to get pictures of our fishing activities, presumably to take back and show their American friends. Well, we oblige them at every opportunity because they promise to send us a few snaps after the film is developed. They take snaps of father and mother on the stage-head, me pronging fish, Bill and Albert doing the splitting and the rest of my brothers carrying out different tasks. It certainly will be fun for them trying to explain to their friends back in the States some of the utensils we use. Take for instance the canvas-lined hook and lead box for our cod jiggers and dabbers, the crude fish-splitting table, the canvas-lined grub box made from an old butter tub, and the rickety looking stage in which they stand. They also take snaps of Bessie and Lill standing by the shack and the flake with young Walt turning over a few fish. Everything is being captured on camera including our black, brown, and white dog Sport, seafarers Daisy and Rosie, and even Pawk in his pen. Nobody is being left out of this 'snapshot panorama,' as they call it. It will be a great story of their visit to the Island.

Mother, of course invites them in for a cup of tea. They appreciate the hospitality and keep her busy answering questions about our fishing operation. She also takes them around the Island to visit a few other shacks and introduce them.

We wonder why anyone would want to capture us through the medium of photography and we are all a little shy about posing. They don't relent on their photo opportunity and their cameras are even busy as they leave port and set a course for town again, waving profusely until out of sight and we are all waving too.

There is not much more work to be done today except to secure the fish on the flakes. Father tells me to stay ashore and help with that while he, Bill and George attend to the nets. A few dark clouds are evident over the eastern horizon and he wants to make sure the fish are all gathered because of potential rain showers. He turns out to be right, and about an hour later we witness a few late afternoon showers as we scramble to get the fish under cover.

When father and the boys return, we find out that the net had less than a quintal of fish and that doesn't take too long to handle. It disappears almost as fast as I can prong it up on the stage-head. We did have a few mackerel in our other net that we will use for bait, although Bill has salted a few for cooking later. Mother usually takes advantage of fresh mackerel for boiling, and maybe tomorrow that is what we will have for dinner. Nothing left now except a mug-up and then 'hit the sack.'

I think about the events of the day and the excursion to the Island by the Tapp family. How different their life must be compared to ours. Would my family have a chance to travel and learn more about other places, or will this be our whole life? More particularly, would I be able to go away and visit back home as a tourist with nice clothes not made from flour sacks or handed down from older brothers? I envisage such a life as I proceed into dreamland.

Basic Sustenance

I never see any food wasted here by our family. There are so many mouths to feed that no food is left over to spoil and everything is eaten as it is prepared. Bread and potatoes with fish are the staples in our diet along with the fresh milk from the goats. During the summer there is a gradual supply of vegetables including carrots, turnips, parsnips, cabbage, beets, dandelions and rhubarb, as they reach harvest stage.

Mother's daily menu for the cooked meal at noontime is the same for each week. All we have to do is remember the day of the week and we know the food to expect. She cooks with economy in mind and a touch that produces food with fine flavour, at least I think so, and the way it disappears all the other family members must think the same way.

Our weekly midday menu runs something like this. On Sunday, jiggs' dinner is the main course. This is a mixture of vegetables, boiled and flavoured with salt pork and salt beef. Since it is a special day of rest, mother usually throws in something extra like a rice pudding, gingerbread, or a molasses duff. Then on Monday we have leftovers from the big jigs dinner the day before. Sometimes this is in the form of hash, where the vegetables are cut up in small pieces or mashed and onion added for the flavour. This I find delicious. Tuesday it is boiled beans. Mother puts the beans 'in soak' the night before to soften them. They are sure good with the fresh bread and sometimes I add a smidgen of molasses. Wednesday is brain-food day, fish. This meal takes many forms and might be cods' tongues, stewed whole fish, fried fillets, britches, cods' heads, salt cod, capelin, herring, mackerel or salmon. Jiggs' dinner appears once more on Thursday, but not as elaborately done as on Sunday and no extras. Friday is fish day again and it will consist of a different meal than we had on Wednesday. We end up on Saturday with pea soup and dumplings. Those dumplings are mainly flour and water, but when soaked in the soup they sure help to fill your stomach. The soup is also flavoured with small pieces of salt beef. So that is the week's menu prepared by mother, Bessie, and Lill.

Readily it can be seen that fish and vegetables are used extensively as food items. They are relatively cheap because we catch the fish and we grow most of our own vegetables. The soil provides us with food while the sea provides us with food and money. However, I often heard father and the other men talk about years when the voyage was poor and money was really scarce. They said that the vegetables and fish had to be rationed throughout the winter to keep the family from starving. Sometimes they even denied themselves the salted fish because it was sold in order to get money for other items really needed. On many occasions, 'lassy bread' and tea became a full meal. Must have been tough and I'm sure glad I was not a part of it, at least so far. No need for me to worry my little head about that this year because our cod catches have been good.

The heat in the shack in the summertime when mother and the girls are preparing dinner on the Ideal Cook stove is sometimes overcoming. It is necessary because heat is required to obtain hot water for washing, baking bread and for cooking. However, washing and the baking of bread are done early in the day when it is usually not so hot. Needless to say, as little time as possible is spent in the shack during the summer and I am usually out in the boat fishing anyhow.

The teapot is continuously on the stove. Everyone loves tea and it is the only beverage except for goats' milk. We have tea for breakfast, dinner, supper, and mug-ups. If anyone visits, conversation takes place with a cup of tea. Orange pekoe is most common and usually comes from Ceylon which is part of the Commonwealth. I see the odd wooden tea crate in retail stores in town with Ceylon marked on it. This sometimes gets my mind thinking as I try to figure out in my own way how tea from such a faraway land can reach us here in Newfoundland. I also try to understand at the same time how fish from the Island can end up on someone's plate in Italy or Brazil. I often watch schooners loaded with salted fish pass the Island, sailing for distant shores with only the compass to use for navigation, and it is difficult to comprehend that they can find places across the Atlantic or in the Caribbean.

Fruit is an unknown quantity except for wild fruit like currants, blueberries, blackberries, partridge berries, and gooseberries, although we have the occasional apple or orange. During summer and until a new crop is ready, mother uses the preserves prepared in the previous fall. The variety of items like buns, cakes, pies, and duffs that can be made from berries add to our culinary treats. Molasses and raisins are also cheap and available so we have abundant molasses and raisin buns and cookies.

I like it when mother asks me to go to the store in town to buy a gallon of molasses. Most of all, I like watching my gallon bottle being filled with the molasses from the big puncheon and then sliding my fingers across the top of the bottle to taste the drippings. Father obtains an empty puncheon now and again and most often there is still a little molasses left in the bottom that he manages to save. The puncheon is valuable to us for curing our fish and we have a number of them in the stage.

I don't see any written recipes for anything that mother cooks. She either remembers it or makes it up on the spur of the moment. I have heard her talk with other women and they sometimes trade ideas about how to cook certain foods. Consequently, the only way Bessie and Lill can learn is by watching and remembering and their memories appear to be good. I'm glad I don't have to remember the recipes, or cook either. Oh well, time for a cup of tea to wash down another one of those molasses buns.

As I continue to mature, I find that mother always has what I would consider an appropriate saying to fit many of the occasions where I am involved. For instance, if it looks like I am taking more than my fair share of food she says, "You for yourself and God for us all."

If I ask her to do something that I can easily do myself she says, "God helps those who help themselves."

Likewise, if I tell her I want to do something because one of my friends is doing it, she casually says, "If he jumped over the wharf, would you want to do it, too?"

It is difficult I confess, to argue with her logic, and I suppose there is a lesson to be learned from each of her sayings. I pay attention, but there are a few sayings that she has to repeat over and over. It seems that the older I get, the more I hear them.

End of Summer

The cod-trap fishery has come to an end for the Noels and Frenches in particular, who depend more on that method of fishing. Capelin schools have long gone and the cod have dispersed too. It is when the cod are chasing the capelin that cod traps are more effective. However, although the cod-trap fishery has ended for this season, the fishery still continues.

Another sign of the ebbing summer is the appearance of mackerel. Sometimes schools of mackerel can be seen breaching the surface as they move around the bay. These sleek and slender fish are powerful swimmers and are also tasty when cooked. There does not seem to be as many mackerel around this year compared to last year. For some reason according to father, there are years when they fail to put in an appearance at all. Anyway, enough about that, I'm only interested in catching them when they do show up in our waters.

The warm breezes of summer transgress into stronger, cooler winds as days continually shorten, signifying the approach of fall. Nights are cooler and the morning sun takes longer to heat the land. Clouds are more frequent and heavier, blocking out the sun more often. However, father contends that with less humidity, this is excellent drying weather for our fish.

We spend the next few days sorting the fish as best we can, according to their moisture content. Experience is required to be able to estimate the moisture content just by feeling the fish, and I have not reached that stage of apprenticeship yet. Texture of the fish is of great concern and father always has the last say on quality.

Father exhibits some pride because we are one of the high-liners amongst fishing crews on the Island. The covered flakes and fish in the stage attest to our success. And the voyage isn't over yet, for we still have the fall fishery ahead of us. This year will be better than last year and it means more fish to sell plus more fish for our own use. Father said he will take a small quantity back to town for sale to retailers during the late fall and winter in order to obtain extra spending money. All appears good.

CHAPTER NINE

Squid-Jigging

Although we are presently using gillnets and hand-lines to catch cod, father now turns to baited trawls. This is a fishery I enjoy, except for the jigging of squid for bait. Squid-jigging has to be the dirtiest part of fishing. The red squid jiggers do a good job of attracting the fish, but when you haul them up and they break the surface of the water, the squids are not particular where they shoot their inky discharges that we refer to as 'squid juice.'

Squids are strange animals of the sea. They have an ink sac that they use for defence by squirting ink at predators to aid their escape. The eight tentacles protruding from their heads have suction cups to hold prey, and they have a beak like a bird at the base. Anyone who has been bitten by a squid can attest to the effectiveness of the beak, and I have had first-hand experience many times. They also have the ability to swim backward as well as forward, or as we like to say, they have reverse gear. Another distinguishing feature is the ability to change colour from reddish to almost translucent, the latter most likely a natural attribute to enable them to approach prey undetected and is a camouflage against predators. Since squid do not have any backbone, but only two strips of cartilage called 'pens' down their sides, they can be easily grabbed by predators. We remove those pens when preparing squid for cooking.

I have heard and read about giant squid, some of it is fiction and some is true. I suppose it is true that it is the largest animal without a backbone on this earth. My teacher told us that one of the biggest ever recorded was caught off Newfoundland in 1878 that had a total tentacle and body length of fifty-two and one-half feet. Awesome, I wouldn't want to catch one like that on my squid-jigger.

Squid-jigging is often a late-evening affair. The more squid-jigging boats you can get in one place, the better your chances to get a good catch. Father usually leaves the squid-jigging to Bill, Albert, or George, but I often join them. Sometimes we jig for squid for two hours or more and not catch one, then all of a sudden they strike and you can fill the boat.

This particular evening we are off Halfway Point along with a number of other boats from the Island as well as from Harbour Grace. George, Albert, and I have been designated to try and jig squid for bait to use the next day. After about an hour on the scene it is getting very tiresome, letting the jiggers go down and hauling them up again without a squid to show for the effort. Sure enough, next thing I hear is the squirting sound of a squid as Mr. John Noel hauls up the first one in his boat a few fathoms away from ours. Pretty soon all hands are standing up in their boats, and the sounds of squirting squids fill the air. It seems that when one person catches a squid, everybody starts hauling them in over the side.

I don't understand why it is, but many times when George jigs a squid the accompanying squirt often hits me. I'm not sure if this is coincidental either, as there seems to be a slight grin on George's face even though he tries his best to conceal it. The enthusiasm of squid-jigging provokes a little fun, and since I am the youngest, why not put me through the ropes as part of my squid-jigging training. An indoctrination of sorts and a little fun for my older brothers.

As I mentioned, squid-jigging is the messiest job in the whole fishing business. I have squid juice on me everywhere. It is up the sleeves of my oilskin jacket, down my neck and all over my face. The taste of that stuff is not too pleasant either. For the novice, it can be an unheralded experience. One thing I found out you must never do when jigging squid, and that is to look over the gunnel of the boat to see if the squid is almost up to the surface of the water. Very often this leads to a full squirt in the face, as the squid reaches the surface and sprays the inky fluid. Now, how do you think I know this? Of course, we have devised a clever means to eliminate such situations from happening, at least most of the time. It entails tying a small knot in the line above the jigger so that when your hand hits it while hauling up the line, you know the jigger is almost to the gunnel and you can govern yourself accordingly which means moving backward a short distance. However, as mentioned earlier, very often you are hit with the squid juice from squids being hauled up by other persons in the boat or even from another boat.

As the red western sky vanishes into night, we decide our squid catch is sufficient for the next day's baiting. Albert hoists the grapnel and George takes the oars and points our boat in the direction of home.

On arrival at the stage, we unload the squids and clean off the squid juice using salt water. Oilskins have to be cleaned completely and hung up to dry for next day. Father is there with the lantern to provide light for our final chores. After about a half hour, we are in the shack for another wash with fresh, warm water and then a mug-up before bedtime.

Hook-and-Line Trawling

We arise very early and in the lantern light we undertake the task of baiting the trawls for the first time this season using the squids we had jigged last evening. Trawl-baiting is a three-man operation if time is to be reduced. Albert cuts the squids into bait-sized pieces, George baits the hooks with the squid pieces, and Bill coils the trawl into the tub. It is a four-man operation if you want to count me for passing the squids to Albert for the cutting procedure.

Longline trawls are employed by crews in the fall after the cod have gone through their period of glutting themselves on capelin. The cod grow rapidly because of abundance of prey and are now in prime condition. Following this earlier encounter with capelin, they are starting to get really hungry again. Squid is a priority bait for cod, especially after the capelin have moved from inshore waters. If squids show up in the bays in copious numbers, then codfish may often be present inshore as well before they migrate to deeper water. We anticipate the codfish are still around.

Trawling is an efficient way of covering a large area of fishing ground. One trawl-line is fifty fathoms in length, and attached to it are 'sud-lines,' that have hooks on the ends. Those hooks are baited with squid, herring, or mackerel, but squid is the preferred bait because it stays on the hooks longer and is considered to be more durable. Sud-lines are one fathom long and are attached to the main trawl line at one-fathom intervals. The hooks have an eye in the top through which the loop made in the sud-line is passed and then down over the hook to complete the attachment, much the same way as you attach a trout hook to a line. Through simple mathematics, it can be determined that each trawl line has fifty hooks. The hooks we use are 'Mustad,' and the box says they came from Norway. The hooks are often referred to as 'banker hooks' because they are also used by fishermen who fish from banking schooners.

The trawls are kept in trawl tubs that are most often sawed-off flour barrels. Father has joined five trawl-lines together in each tub, which amounts to two hundred and fifty hooks and is over a quarter mile long.

Baited trawls when set out on the fishing grounds are anchored and buoyed at each end. Attached to the buoy is a 'high-flyer,' which is a flag marked with the initials of the skipper of the fishing crew and in our case it shows the marking TS. These high-flyers make it possible to find the trawl more easily and it allows other skippers to know you have a trawl set in the area. However, it sometimes happens that one fishing crew could set their trawl across another already set. I did experience one instance when we hauled our trawl to find another had been set across it. In order to untangle it, we had to pass our trawl underneath the other and let the other one go while continuing to haul ours. Luckily, this cross-over of trawls does not happen very often because most skippers know the fishing grounds and have knowledge of where and how each skipper usually sets his trawls. Crews often use compass bearings to set the trawls and this helps to keep them apart.

Dawn arrives about the time we have the trawls baited and placed aboard the punt. Father has put the necessary fishing equipment in the boat and we are soon underway. Other crews are also on the water and heading in various directions, some of them close to us. Last night, father decided that Eastern Rock would be our general direction. With the bright morning sun in the eastern sky, we row directly into the dancing rays as they give the surface of the water a reddish-gold appearance.

Very soon the first grapnel is tossed overboard and heading toward the bottom, along with the inside end of the trawl, followed by the high-flyer to act as the mark on the surface. Father has already made visual markings as well as compass bearings to help us locate the trawl later. He plays out the trawl from the tub as we take turns rowing slowly in an easterly direction. Every now and again father holds the trawl steady, for a tug on the line indicates that fish are taking the trawl bait. The breeze from the southeast has increased a little bit since sun-up, but is still very moderate. As the last end of the trawl approaches, George prepares to let the other grapnel go overboard with another high-flyer to mark our outside end. Now all we can do is await the anticipated results and hope the cod will be encouraged to eat our squid bait.

We row a little to the northwest, and at last out comes the 'caboose.' Soon we have the kettle boiling for a cup of tea to wash down our lassy bread. I have also brought along a few dried capelin that I cook over the open fire, browning them slightly on each side. However, the odd one develops a more black-looking appearance, since it is a tricky situation trying to direct the heat properly as we rock back and forth in the boat. I eat a black one to show I am tough and can handle rough food. The taste of the salt in the capelin masks the burnt taste to a small degree, although it is still very pronounced.

While waiting to haul the trawl, we prepare individual hand-lines. If we can catch any fish on hand-lines, it may mean we will do well with the trawls. Hand-lines are about thirty fathoms in length but can go to fifty fathoms. They have a hook attached on each end, to which bait is applied. A lead weight is attached above the hook to act as a sinker. The line is coiled on a reel that is rectangular and made with four pieces of wood. The reels are an effective method for storing the hand-lines and are easy to use.

We bait the hand-lines with pieces of squid and lower them until the lead hits the bottom. Then, hauling up about a fathom to prevent tangling in the bottom, we sit and dangle the lines over the side and wait for hungry cod.

A couple of hours pass and the hand-lines have not produced much of a catch and we only have about a dozen fish for our efforts. Father finally decides that we will now begin to haul the trawl as he turns the boat toward the direction of our inside buoy. Before long Bill is snagging the line on the high-flyer with the fish-gaff and taking it on board, and that is followed by the retrieval of the grapnel. We now begin the process of hauling the trawl.

Hook by hook the trawl comes aboard and is coiled in the tub. Fish are scarce. We get four or five cod on consecutive hooks and then go probably twenty hooks or more with neither one. The size of the cod is not a problem but quantity is. By the time we have hauled the last hook there are roughly three quintals in the mid-ship-room of the boat. Apart from the cod we encounter a few skate and sculpins. Father rationalizes that it may be a bit early for trawling yet. He explains, "There is a strong tide and that may indicate a storm is brewing. A stir-up is needed to get the cod moving again and after that it may mean more success with the trawl."

It appears as if he is giving us some of his reasoning for the poor catch today while at the same time reassuring us for better catches later. Nobody argues his point.

At least this year our trawl fishery is not interrupted as it was last year. I remember hauling the trawl last September when suddenly every hook coming into view had a shark on it, dogfish shark that is. One after another we hauled the sharks in, removed the hooks, and threw them overboard. I have heard father talk about the scourge of dogfish and now I know what he meant. We have to be careful in freeing them from the hooks because their teeth are really sharp and the gaff has to be used on each one. I also know from previous conversations that it is useless to continue trawling while dogfish are in the area. All they do is gobble our bait and present us with the time-consuming problem of hauling them aboard the boat, and prying them off the hooks. Dogfish sharks are of no use to us and are a real nuisance since we have no buyer for them, but I have read that they are eaten in some parts of the world. To me, a fish has to look good before I will eat it, and dogfish do not fit that description. Then again, I may make exception on occasion because squid are not enticing-looking creatures either, and I eat them.

Conversation on the way back to the Island is brief. This often happens when fish catches are small and enthusiasm wanes. The remainder of our fishing colleagues did not fare much better than us, as we learn upon landing. After processing the catch it is time to forget about today and look forward to tomorrow. Fish travel in schools and we trust that in the days ahead they will enter our area in more abundance. Even though father has knowledge of our fishing grounds, the fish still have to decide to swim our way. If they show up we will catch them, but if they don't then our trawl fishery for this year will be modest.

Mother has cookies and molasses buns on the table as I enter the shack door. I know what I will have for my mug-up tonight.

The Blow

It appears as if father is right. The early morning sky is starting to show signs of forthcoming inclement weather. Flickering lantern light is seen in the stages, but crews are there more from habit than a determination to actually go fishing today. The undertow is strong and causes splashes of water on the headlands, even though the wind is only moderate. Daylight starts to show and appears to be much slower than usual in arriving. The whole sky does not have that familiar appearance. Fishermen visit from stage to stage and discuss the potential weather. The consensus is to refrain from going to sea today and to secure our fishing premises in preparation for what is expected. As daylight overtakes us, the sun's infrequent rays produce awe-inspiring colours as they break through the clouds, only to be engulfed by heavy clouds again that move swiftly across the sky. It gives the impression that the clouds are fighting to keep the sun from shining. I peer at the sky and listen to the interpretations of the weather coming from father and the other men. This is a learning process and I am about to learn more about weather predictions from looking at the sky.

Father soon tells us, "Secure the punt on the launch-way, but haul it up farther than normal as an extra precaution. You can help some of the others haul up their boats too."

We all chip in and soon our punt is considered to be on safe ground. In order to provide added safety, we attach a line around the stem-head of the boat and tie it to a large, immoveable rock on land. All items in the punt are removed and stored in the stage. We have encountered storms in the past and we trust this one will not be any more detrimental.

Having completed that job, we go back to the shack for breakfast. A familiar smell hits my nostrils, as mother has just finished kneading the dough for another batch of her fabulous bread. She covers it and places it aside to rise before shaping it into buns for baking. The Ideal Cook is pouring out the heat, and the teapot is full and ready. I cut a couple of slices of bread off a loaf from mother's previous batch and put them on a wire rack over the stove to toast. Since we have plenty of time this morning, the toast and jam will be a real treat.

Outside the sun's rays are penetrating the clouds in sporadic bursts before being concealed again by more swiftly moving clouds. Although there is plenty of movement in the sky, the sea remains relatively calm, but the water looks black. The intenseness of the low cloud cover reflects over the water, giving it the dark appearance. Even though there are abundant clouds, there is no rain or fog. I am hearing the older folks say that this is not the type of sky conditions they encounter very often.

Next order of business for us is the stage, where some of our salted fish is stored. I place a wooden cover over the hole in the floor of the stage. We use that hole to dump the fish guts and sound-bones from our processing operation into the water below. I also put a killick on the cover to keep it in place. Father uses a few large sticks to brace the stage door from potential winds. He certainly does not want any damage done to the salted fish inside. We all hope the stage itself can withstand what is about to come.

In the meantime there are fish on the flakes in various phases of drying. We gather this dried and partially dried codfish and put it in bulks before covering with canvas tarps. Rocks are put on the edges of the tarps and on the top of each pile to hold them in place. We all continue with various tasks as the sky remains threatening, with the wind gradually picking up and not abating as it normally does. Whatever kind of storm is coming, it is really taking a long time to develop. Slowly and methodically, sky, wind, waves and tides are unfolding in a combination of nature's powers against what we are doing in an effort to resist. Man against the elements, and father isn't taking any chances.

We spend the afternoon picking up or tying down anything that could potentially blow away. Father and mother discuss various items that have to be protected, and we act appropriately to their wishes. Other families on the Island are also taking similar precautions. Everyone is expecting the worst.

The setting sun is out of sight to us except for infrequent bursts of orange colour penetrating through the heavy, mingling clouds in the western sky. During the last hour there have been occasional rain showers, but of short duration. As nightfall overtakes the Island, no stars are visible and it is as dark as pitch. We settle down in the shack listening to the sounds of the increasing wind as it picks up momentum and rain finally starts to pelt our roof. The sea can be heard pounding in the Launch Way as the rising tide helps to increase the power of the incoming waves. Father anxiously ventures out the door periodically to observe conditions and get his own status of the weather. Each time he does so, the wind circulates through the shack and interferes with the glow from the lamps. There is little else that can be done for the night so one by one we find our beds and slowly go to sleep lulled by the sounds of the sea, the wind, and the rain.

In the early morning hours the wind and the rain pound the Island. It is difficult to sleep. Even Sport sleeps with one eye open. He tends to spend a lot of time walking between bedrooms as though he is checking on everyone to see if they are okay. Each unusual sound from outside is interpreted to be something blowing around or blown down. Leaks begin appearing in our roof, and a few pots and pans are used to catch the falling water. Father and mother could barely be heard as they quietly check conditions in the shack and casually glance in our direction to investigate our welfare. Occasionally voices can be heard outside as neighbouring families deal with their own situations. It is one of those nights when you go to bed, but don't get much sleep.

As night wears on, curiosity prompts and forces me to look ahead as to what the daylight will bring. I can tell from my parent's conversations that apprehension was prevailing in their minds too. They speak about the shack, the boat, the flakes and the weather. Even though they are concerned, they also try to use reassuring words for our benefit.

The long night is finally ending and daylight stares in through our kitchen windows to pierce the darkness and allow us visibility for another day. Oddly enough too, the wind and rain start to lose their noisy embrace with only intermittent bursts of power. However, when it appears that weather conditions are abating, a sudden gust of wind starts everything shaking again. Soon we are all on deck and dressed in eager anticipation of what lay ahead. The pots and pans are still employed to catch the leaks from the roof. At least we still have a roof.

Mother and father give us younger ones instructions as to what to do and what not to do. Father, Bill, and Albert dress in their oilskins and go outside to do the first inspection, along with Sport of course. Shortly thereafter the door opens slightly, and father pokes his head in to tell mother the stovepipe is fine and a fire can be lit, but to make only a small fire until the weather improves. For me that means we will soon get breakfast, and finally get a little heat because the rain has given the shack a feeling of dampness.

I look out the front and back kitchen windows to make my own observations, along with Bob and Walt. Bessie and Lill are still in their own bedroom keeping themselves busy at something until mother calls them to help with breakfast. The sky still contains those fast-moving, blackish clouds like those seen yesterday, interspersed with faint orange colour now in the eastern sky. The darker clouds mask the rising sun and it gives the impression of lights getting bright and then being dimmed again. The inclement weather is ending the same way it had begun, slowly and methodically. I see small groups of men walking from place to place, shack to shack, as they survey each family's situation as to the extent of damage, if any. My view through the windows is rather obscured and I long to get out and see for myself.

Just as the girls are announcing the first evidence of breakfast, father and the boys return. Throughout the breakfast conversation we find out the news of the storm damage as it applies to all the Island families. A couple of shacks have chimneys blown off and a few sustained roof damage when felt was torn off by the wind. Many shacks had leaks like we had. All stages and boats are safe with only minor instances of damage. Safety of the boats is a prime concern because the fishing season is not over yet. Father and the other men have satisfied themselves that this storm must have been the tail end of a hurricane that started down south and worked its way up the eastern seaboard. It definitely is not the normal type of storm we associate with in these parts. The intensity of the wind and the ominous sky leading up to the storm were unusual, as is the departure of the storm clouds today.

I realize how helpless we are here in Conception Bay. Nothing to do when a storm approaches but prepare as best we can and ride it out. Our Island is like a ship on the high seas with nowhere to go because when a storm starts, we are stuck. As well as being physically isolated, we have an isolated feeling too. Our family, along with the other families, learn to take what comes and rather than fight it, we live with it. It is a way of life, and for the most part we enjoy the freedom, such as it is.

For the remainder of the morning and early afternoon hammers can be heard as shack repairs are made and the fences restored to a vertical position. Flakes lost some of the spruce boughs that covered the tops and they have to be retrieved later today, most likely by the younger ones like me. I think about the massive strength of the sea as I listen to the strong undertow rumbling in and out of the coves and splashing off the rocks and headlands. Our flimsy looking stage survived last night's ordeal mainly due to its type of structure. Stages like ours are not built to withstand seas, but rather to exist with them. The foundation is such that seas can move around them freely without too much resistance. Some enterprising fisherman without an engineering degree had probably figured this out many years ago and we were simply capitalizing on his expertise.

A storm can have certain advantages for us and our surroundings. For instance, the stage floor is completely washed clean, but our salted fish is left untouched. The boards in the stage floor allowed some salt water to penetrate through and swirl around before draining back through again. Also, our cove which was full of fish guts is now completely clean through the action of the waves and tide. Anything on the Island that was not nailed down was blown away, but that was very little. As the sun peeked from the clouds later, there seemed to be a new freshness associated with the cleansing action of the storm. A new freshness and vitality to an old traditional way of life of which I am a part.

The storm didn't stop Rosie and Daisy from producing milk. They huddled beside the lee side of the shack out of the wind to protect themselves from much of the driving rain.

Pawk is okay as well, but then I didn't expect wind and rain would have very much of an effect on a gull. Their feathers must be an excellent type of protective covering from wind, rain, and cold because they spend all their time on the seashore regardless of weather. I ponder this while looking at Pawk standing there as if to say, what is all the fuss about? I have not learned of any other creature that has feathers, apart from a bird. Feathers are the one distinguishing feature and it is obvious they provide good insulation against the elements.

There is a sense of uneasiness among many people after this storm. Assurances are given to help bring back and maintain the contentment that was previously prevalent. Visits are planned to go to town to assess any damage that may have occurred there, although it would be a couple of days before the seas calm down to allow boats to leave. There is still a lot of undertow remaining as a result of the storm.

For me and my friends the storm was another experience and in many ways broke the monotony. At least there is no severe fallout and life is already back to resembling normal. Of course, normal here might not be considered normal by many people. The only normal things I do are go to sleep and wake up, and both of these daily events I consider as joyous occasions.

Suppertime provides a period of reflection and an expression of thankfulness for the way we have endured the past night. It is "thank God for this and thank God for that," as individual family members bring up the various things that could have happened. Father takes time to tell us of other storms similar to this one that he has witnessed, sometimes with more disastrous results. He said, "I remember when a storm ten years ago damaged a number of boats and two crews had to cut short their fishing season because it was too late in the year to make repairs and get back fishing. There was another year when wind persisted for about three days after a storm and nobody could leave the Island. Unfortunately, one fisherman while making repairs to his shack, fell and injured his head only to pass away on the Island before medical help could be obtained. It was a dreadful loss for that family, and so much so that neither of his two sons wanted to take over their father's fishing operation."

While everyone is busy talking, I help myself as best I can to available food. Mother decides that because of the storm she will cook our main meal for supper. Tonight's special is roasted rounders and along with a bit of butter, they are very satisfying when accompanied by a few boiled potatoes and fresh bread. Yes, Wednesday again and we are still sticking to the same weekly menu. It would take more than a storm for mother to change our eating habits. I have been indulging in more than my share and that prompted mother to quote one of her religious sayings, "You for yourself and God for us all."

Winding Down

The aftermath of the storm keeps us from fishing for a couple of days. During this time we tend more to the fish-drying process by turning them over more frequently during the day. The wind is brisk each day and this helps considerably. Father, along with Bill and George spend a lot of their efforts ensuring the dryness of the fish and grading each fish as best they can by quality and size. Albert and Bob tend to the flakes and carry the fish to them for culling.

We still have vegetables growing here on the Island, even though the garden has provided us with fresh produce for well over a month. By the time we leave there will be very little remaining.

I am left to tend to a few chores in the stage. Apart from the salted fish that we produce, there are a number of other items that we get from the cod. Not much of our cod catches are wasted because in the stage we have processed salted-sounds, heads, tongues, chitlins and peas. I have worked hard to get those products ready for use over the coming fall and winter. Sounds are delicious when mother makes them into hash in the frying pan along with potatoes and onions that are seasoned with pepper. Heads are prepared for food by removing the gills and eyes and then splitting them so that they lay flat for salting. The cooked fried-heads are eaten by sucking the fish flesh from the bones. Tongues are cut from the heads and provide a boneless item of distinct sweet taste when fried with scrunchions. Some people don't like the 'jelly-like' part of the tongue, but I like to just suck in that part and let it slip down my throat. Chitlins are often mixed with the sounds in hash. Peas, or britches as some people call them, are fried or baked in the oven and are a real delicacy when served with mustard or some of mother's pickles. I even hear tell of people frying the gills of cod, but not us. However, some of us may pop codfish eyes in our mouths just to show off in front of the girls. When you think of it, the lowly cod has much to offer in variety of food products. For us, the cod means survival in more ways than one.

The oncoming cooler, shorter days and longer nights with more frequent rain showers have coalesced to give us the onset of fall. We tend to slow down with the season. Father is more contented after this season because the voyage has been good, and we have some fishing time remaining. However, we are still pursuing the fishery using hand-lines and trawls, and he is just as determined to get a good catch as he was earlier.

One bright, cool day we set our trawl with the inside buoy just east of Salvage Rock and running seaward through the deeper ship's channel. Squids are used as bait. Rather than leave the trawl to fish for a few hours, father decides it might be better to under-run it. Picking up the inside buoy, Bill begins the process. This entails hauling the trawl up to the boat, removing the fish, if any, baiting the hooks when necessary, and lowering it to the bottom again. In reality, the boat actually runs beneath the trawl, hence the term under-running. It is a good way to fish in some respects because if fish are plentiful in the area, you can fish it over and over again. Fish are very spotty today, however, especially on the inside part of the trawl, so we abandon any more under-running and let the trawl rest on the bottom for a while.

How different it is in the fall in comparison to the summer. The winds are stronger and the seas heavier as they hit the boat and fly off in a complete spray rather than mist. The water takes on a more mystical nature. You have to be more careful in the boat to avoid falling or getting tossed overboard.

I remember the superstitions laid down by father as to what to do, and what not to do, while in the boat. I'll never forget the first time I whistled. The tone in father's voice when he bawled out to tell me to stop whistling entrenched in me forever that I was not to do it again. Another habit I had to learn was to always turn the boat with the movement of the sun and never against it. I couldn't figure out the difference, the boat seemed to turn just as well either way. It is an example of working in harmony with nature rather than against it. Those heavenly bodies like the sun are not to be antagonized in any way.

Fall fishing when catches are smaller is a time to obtain a supply of fish mainly for our own use. The smaller daily catches can be easily handled even though we have shorter daylight hours to work. The few quintals that father cures in the fall will see us through the winter. However, he usually sells the best and keeps the worst.

Time to tend the trawl, so George and Bill row toward the inside buoy and we are soon in the process of hauling it, hook by hook and line by line. It is fun watching the gleaming white stomachs of cod as they come into view from the depths. The more white stomachs you can see, the better the fishing.

Then something appears on the water ahead of us as my eyes scan over the horizon. At first I thought it was a wave breaking on the surface. "What is that floating on the surface?" I ask.

Father's trained eyes look in the direction of my pointing finger and without much hesitation says, "It's a fish that has come afloat on the trawl. Sometimes large cod when caught on the trawl tend to fight their way to the surface of the water and take in air."

As we get nearer and nearer I can see it is a large cod. Shortly, Albert has the fish gaffed by the head and he and Bill are hauling it aboard. How big it looks to me as it lets out scary, groaning sounds in the boat. It is the biggest I have ever seen. Thirty pounds? Forty pounds? I couldn't wait to get back and show off this codfish. It doesn't take us too long to haul the rest of the trawl and we are on our way. I keep staring at the big fish all the way to the stage.

Once the punt is secured we haul the large cod up over the stage-head on a rope. A few onlookers appear on the scene to marvel at the large fish. Father weighs the cod on the spring balance and says it is forty-eight pounds. After some excitement, the large fish is split and salted separately in one corner of the stage. How much bigger it looks compared to the other salted fish.

After that bit of excitement, we soon settle down to a feed of stuffed squid. Mother had managed to sneak a few from our bait box last night to prepare for tonight's supper. Bessie and Lill removed the heads and guts and the tough layer of outer skin over the bodies. The stuffing smells and tastes good with the savoury seasoning. Mother has done a good job again, because if cooked too long, squid can be tough. I cut mine in small pieces across the body to make them easier to eat. The sweetness of the squid combined with the tasty stuffing is a real treat and something different.

Dealing with Tragedy

The next day starts out windy, and father assures us it may be best to stay ashore today. Albert and I work in the stage separating our winter's supply of salted products and putting them in containers for the voyage home at a later date.

In the evening hours, accompanied by Sport, I travel to the western edge of the Island to have a look around. Finding a suitable perch on a rock, I sit down and look out toward town. Sport really enjoys hunting which is his area of expertise and he senses that the partridge hunting season is approaching. You can say he has a nose for it.

I think about one time last fall when Sport and I went partridge hunting along the ridge on the south side of Lady Lake. We were walking along slowly when suddenly he froze in his tracks with his tail pointing out behind him. Looking back at me, I knew it was time to get my forefinger ready on the trigger of the shotgun. Then at his next dedicated movement forward, up came a covey of partridge from a small depression behind a rock. I fired. Two birds fell to the ground and the other three flew out of sight around a clump of shrub-trees.

I recollected in my mind the sight of those two dead birds and somehow it triggered my thoughts about another death that still haunts my memory. An agonizing death that was near and dear to me, and I suppose will always be lurking in my memory.

It was the summer of 1916 when I was only eight. Sister Winnie, Walt, and I came down with the measles and a few other families on the Island were also afflicted. As was customary, mother placed all three of us in a darkened bedroom and she became our full-time nurse, never leaving our sides. Winnie was only two and appeared to be suffering the greatest. I suppose her age meant that more care was required because she was too young to really speak for herself. Constantly mother tended us as we went through periods of sleep, wakefulness, and suffering. I observed the red circular marks covering my body and prayed for them to disappear.

I don't know who got the measles first, but it must have spread quickly. I became aware when my nose wouldn't stop running and my head became hot before becoming full of red spots. Mother used the word contagious and she said we had to be kept isolated.

Day and night mother was on her feet as cries of mom, mom emanated from Winnie's bed. She was careful in caring for us while trying to protect the rest of the family. Now as I think of it, the conditions she had in which to nurse us and keep the family going at the same time demanded extraordinary determination and stamina. It was difficult enough when we were all well. Bill, Albert, and George had the measles a few years ago and mother said they had immunity to it. Bessie and Lill caught them last year, but according to mother they did not suffer too greatly.

Rubbing Sport on the head, I recalled the sounds from little sister Winnie as she lay in her bed. Since she was the smallest, everyone in the family always spent time with her to keep her amused and quiet. Walt was relatively young and she followed him around as best she could, sometimes to her detriment. She shortened his name to 'Alter' because she could pronounce it more easily. Bessie and Lill were around her the most while mother was busy at other things. Her immature years had not yet acknowledged the rigours of life here on the Island so she always appeared happy no matter where she was and what she was doing.

Then one night Winnie's cries suddenly stopped and silence came from her bed. Mother was forever present in the room and I listened as she apparently held Winnie, wrapped in a bedsheet, trying her utmost to hide her deep sorrow and profound loss. Father was saying comforting words with the realization there was nothing more either of them could do, but mother had done her best. As the Scripture says, "In the midst of life, we are in death."

That night was the quietest I have witnessed in our shack. Neither father nor mother came to tell us what had happened, but it was unnecessary anyway. All we did was lie in our bunks and try to absorb what was taking place, knowing we would have to somehow get past it, even though at this moment we were still in the middle of it. Losing a family member is not easy.

I remember the minister coming to the Island to hold the funeral service for Winnie in the kitchen of the shack. The family gathered round and I could hear Bessie and Lill sobbing somewhat uncontrollably. Walt and I were still confined to our beds, but making a recovery and feeling much better. We understood what was happening as we listened to the sombre tone of the proceedings. Somehow my own sickness was secondary to the event taking place. Even now, whenever I hear the hymn that they sang, "Jesus, Friend of Little Children," I remember the very day of the service and the scene in the shack as Winnie, the youngest in our family, left the Island for the last time.

After the service, father and the boys went to Harbour Grace for the burial. Mother was forced to say her final goodbye as the little casket left the kitchen because she felt her obligation to care for us was her duty at this time. There was nothing else she could do for Winnie. I can only imagine what was going through mother's mind at that moment. In her own way, she confined her true feelings and continued to nurse us back to health for the duration of the epidemic.

Gradually the spots disappeared and Walt and I were on the way to full recovery. We regained our strength, as did others on the Island who experienced similar bouts with the measles, but our family suffered the only fatality.

Picking myself up, I feel compassion as Sport leads the way home. I try to think more positive thoughts, but an experience such as the loss of a family member has a habit of clinging to my memory and will always be there.

CHAPTER TEN

End of the Season

The end of the fishing season is both a happy and sad time. Happy due to the fact that another season is over and our voyage this year has been good. Sad because we now have to leave the freedom of the Island way of life and enter a slightly more complex world. Nevertheless, the opportunity to attend school with my friends and learn about new things has a form of spaciousness and anticipation attached to it. The carefree life we enjoy here seems diametrically opposed to our more regimental life in town. In some respects, I suppose town living brings us back to reality.

As I view the surroundings, it reminds me how pleasant it is to live here so close to nature with the birds that can fly to infinity and the fish with their wide-open sea. There are times when I feel just as free as they are. The fresh air fills my nostrils, but is muffled on occasion with the smell of smoke from a nearby chimney. I recall the sounds of gulls hovering around our boat and the roar of the sea during a big undertow. Then there are those mauzy days when the sky appears to be down on top of us and the accompanying nights possess an unforgettable stillness. I reminisce about the summer just past as events run through my mind in no particular order.

Engrossed in the past, I am soon brought to the present by father over at the flakes calling my name. I can tell by the tone that it might be in my best interest to make a quick appearance.

As we gather and sort the salted fish, father supervises and maintains tabs on our activities. Grading the fish calls for experience and sometimes leads to argumentative dialogue. He knows his decisions are not final anyway, for the merchant-buyer will have the last say in regard to quality and price. Regardless, the price never does rise very much but father claims that with good quality, we can at least maintain some sense of fairness. Money is power, and from what I can tell, we don't have it.

The white faces of the salted fish stand out in the bright light of the sun as we go about our business. The uniformity of each lot of fish is becoming more distinct as we separate them by quality and size. Bill and father do most of the grading, although George is very experienced too. I listen to what they are saying to find out the differences in the various quality grades of fish. It appears to me that fish grading is something you learn by making mistakes. You sort of have to look at a fish and weigh the individual merits of it before making a decision. The salt content, moisture content, the splitting, blood spots, texture of the face of the fish, round-tails, thickness of the fish and cuts in the flesh are all considered for quality purposes. I can grade for size, though, because we have the sizes marked on the culling-board. You don't need much education or experience for that.

Mother and the girls have done a good job of rationing the vegetables. Over the next five days we will certainly consume those that remain. We have the harvest from our gardens in town that will provide us with plenty for the winter. Potatoes are the staple and the crop is usually good unless we strike canker. That potato disease can ruin a whole crop. It mainly affects our blue potatoes.

It doesn't seem like five months ago that we were making repairs to the stage in order to get ready for fishing. Now we are concentrating on our departure. This mainly entails securing the facilities because we do not leave any contents of any importance to protect. Fishing gear is prepared for the trip and that will allow father to make repairs to it during the winter. The stage is conditioned and protected, as much as possible, to withstand the ravages of winter and the potential drift ice. One thing about it, I'm glad I don't have to live on the Island during the winter. The lighthouse keeper, Mr. Morris, can keep that job.

Father, George, Bob, and Albert row to town, taking most of the fishing gear with them. There they retrieve our horse, Molly, and bring her home to her barn. She will be needed to haul our fish, fishing gear, and other items after we arrive from the Island. Then later she will plough the potatoes and haul them to the cellar for storage. Bessie and Lill are also in town to get the house ready for us again.

Bill and I remain to help mother make the final preparations in the shack. All our personal belongings are being packed. I will take my entire grooming ensemble, which consists of a comb with about half the teeth missing. Only the bare shack will be left when we are finished. The stove will even be removed, put in the stage, and covered for protection. Mother says the reason for this is to prevent fire. Apparently hunters visit the Island and often use the shack for refuge. There is no harm in hunters using the shack, but without a stove there is less chance of an accidental fire that could burn it down.

It's funny how the shack can be transformed from a place that has vitality to a lonely, barren structure in such a short time. Bessie and Lill have made sure things are packed properly in cardboard boxes. The smell of mother's cooking still leaves a welcome flavour to the place. Tomorrow that will be gone, along with us.

Sport, Walt, and I walk out to where the goats are grazing and we glance around to have our last look on this eve of departure. The footpaths, now well used, will be without footsteps until next spring. Grass will cover the paths in many places as it always has. Some of the neighbouring shacks are already secured and the people are gone. I take my final walk on a few of the paths and end up by my caged gull, Pawk. What is he thinking? I observe that he senses a change and probably wonders what it means for him. His wing feathers are not grown out yet and he is unable to fly. My feathery pet will be accompanying me home.

We walk the path out past Sandy Cove toward Ship Cove to see if father and the boys can be seen on their way back from town. A boat appears in view and as it gets closer I determine it is them. Casually we stroll back and are met by mother, who is looking for young Walt. Sport follows me to the stage as father and the others come into view from around the point.

Mother has mashed up the remaining vegetables for supper as we sit around the table for the last evening meal. Father and mother discuss the remaining items to be attended before making our departure tomorrow. Already they are thinking about the months ahead.

Mother talks about the jams she will make and the fruitcakes to be baked for Christmas. I can make a meal from fruitcake alone and prefer dark cakes over light ones. That's providing I can have a glass of syrup to go with the cake. She will also be taking us to the store to try on new clothes to supplement those she will make herself. Plans are in her mind to put new wallpaper in two of the bedrooms and have the ceilings painted. Looks as if this fall will be a busy one in preparation for the Christmas season.

Father will have plenty to do as well. Some of the trawl lines have to be replaced. Harvesting the vegetables has to be completed before storing them in the cellar. Coal will be bought and stored for use during the winter. Work has to be done on one end of the house which has apparently settled. Father expects he will have to replace some of the wooden foundation. No rest for the weary! I can escape some of the work because I will be in school.

There is one job I know that will test the patience of both mother and father and that is cleaning the chimneys. It appears that no matter how carefully father performs the job, soot still manages to find its way from the kitchen stove to other parts of the kitchen. Cleaning the other chimney that supports our front-room stove does not give the same problem. Albert, George, Bill, and Bob usually find something else to do rather than be around the house during chimney cleaning. They have learned from past experience it is better to leave father and mother alone when this chore is underway.

The process father uses to clean the chimney is a rather crude one and he never falters from it. It involves a length of rope, slightly longer than the chimney is deep, with a piece of rectangular iron tied on one end. He climbs the ladder to the roof and lowers this piece of iron on the rope down the chimney and by repeatedly raising and lowering he tries to dislodge any soot and creosote. He follows this up by taking a long-handled brush, made from pieces of old cloth, and dangles that down and up the chimney to further clean it.

The soot and creosote from the cleaning fall down the chimney, but invariably some of it finds its way out into the stove. Driving a brush down the chimney means that the soot has to go somewhere and the only outlet is through the four covers of the stove. Therefore, much of the soot residue from the chimney ends up in mother's domain, the kitchen.

After father climbs down from the roof, he has to approach the kitchen with some trepidation because he really doesn't know what kind of a mess he will have to contend with apart from a possible verbal outburst from mother. She is always the one doing the talking as father takes the covers from the stove to begin removing the soot and trying as best he can to avoid any spillage. Mother does not leave the kitchen.

After a few snarky remarks from both sides, most of the mess is cleaned up in and around the stove, but Mother realizes that soot has managed to coat other areas away from the stove. She always covers the chairs, dishes, and table with sheets just to be on the safe side, so the damage is not severe. Gradually she tones down somewhat and even begins helping father to move the collected soot and creosote from the kitchen. Some semblance of peace finally returns to our household, and both chimneys have another year's grace.

I think about what I will be doing for the rest of this year. Although I haven't mentioned it yet, there is a strong possibility I may get a job delivering groceries for Mr. Martin Sheppard and helping him in his retail store after school and on Saturdays. I won't know for probably a few weeks yet. Now that I have learned how to take some responsibility, I am anxious to have a job and earn my own money.

Bill, Albert, and George talk about the work left to be done here on the Island. They will be left behind to finish the fish left for our own use and take care of all the last-minute details. One of the last things will be to remove the stove from the shack and secure it in the stage. Father will make one last trip back to ensure everything is secure.

The Departure

Friday dawns early and breakfast is sort of hurried. I am going back today with mother and Walt. On this trip we will take our personal belongings and the animals plus whatever else can be squeezed on board.

After a number of trips from the shack with our personal belongings, the boat is loaded including Rosie, Daisy, Sport, and Pawk. Father must feel a little bit like Noah with all the animals. All we need is the flood.

George and Albert push us off and father takes the oars to begin our journey that may take longer than usual because of the load we have on board. The goats are making a lot of noise, as if they don't want to leave. Pawk too is noisy, but probably for a different reason. He's not sure what is happening because he has no previous experience. I will release him when his feathers are grown back and he can fly, but that will take another couple of weeks yet. My friends in town will get a real kick out of him.

Last night I experienced mixed emotions as I lay in my bunk. While it will be good to get back home, there is enjoyment in my surroundings here as well, even if it is of a different kind. Leaving the Island always has a tinge of sadness attached to it.

I sit down next to Sport near the stern of the boat and look at the Launch Way for the last time. He licks my face affectionately before finding a comfortable place to rest during the ride. Although life may be rugged on the Island, it does bring a measure of accomplishment and tranquility. I treat it as a training ground for the future. I'm sure it includes lessons I will never forget no matter what lies ahead for me.

As we pull away from the stage-head, I realize that the sounds of the Island have disappeared with the people. The hustle and bustle is over. Once more the Island has yielded its harvest and will be left in contentment until next May.

My thoughts turn to home, school, and my friends as the Island slips farther and farther away. The sun breaks through the clouds and casts its rays over the Island as if to give us a last good look. Oars break the water and interrupt the silence. After a half hour or so, I take over the rowing while father mans the sculling oar to keep us on a straight course to Harbour Grace.

I look at mother who also shows a sense of relief in the fact that the fishing season is over and our voyage has been good. She makes small talk as father's big hands drive the sculling oar through the water behind us. His moustache flares as he proudly steers our punt like the coxswain of a whaler to the finish line. I can sense in father the pride of having taken the family through another fishing season safely. The good voyage has given him a feeling of security in regard to having money for the winter ahead. He has experienced much worse situations. His greyish-white hair and sunburned face portray a person who has worked hard and doesn't mind hard work. He often says, "Hard work doesn't hurt anyone." I just wish he wouldn't test that out on me so often just to prove his point.

Soon the sounds of Harbour Grace block out any memory of the Island. The rustle of business activity fills the air. People's voices can be heard as we make our way to the wharf. Father secures our boat at the stern while I secure the bow.

Home again, and another fishing season is under my belt. The tide is about half-up and we begin unloading our cargo as mother jumps ashore and prepares to carry what she can to the house, apart from leading the two goats on a rope. The callousness of my hands reminds me it has not been easy, but that feather mattress is going to feel real soft tonight.

EPILOGUE

Fishermen gradually acquired fishing boats with propulsion engines, sometimes referred to as 'make and break' engines. This type of engine had one cylinder and a large flywheel that was turned by hand to start it. Turning the flywheel started the alternating process of ignition and exhaust that kept the engine running. The spark to ignite the gas was provided by a battery.

Those engines meant that movement to the fishing grounds was faster and residence on the Island was no longer necessary because fishing could take place from Harbour Grace. Also, this kind of fishing life was becoming more uninviting to younger family members. As a result, many sons and daughters emigrated to the Boston area (commonly called the Boston States) or to Montreal to find other types of work.

By the early 1930s, reduced catches of cod along with lower prices for salted fish led many to abandon the summer fishery and opt for work in town. Those remaining in the fishery operated from premises in town. Structures belonging to former Island families were demolished for firewood or sold. No visual traces remain on the Island today of past habitation, and there are few if any records of summer settlement there. This book may be the only information and historical documentation of summer fishing operations on Harbour Grace Island involving family fishing enterprises.

HARBOUR GRACE ISLAND SONG

As Grandfather rocked in his old rocking chair, this story he told us
    one evening
Of the real good old days and those old fishing ways, as he randomly
    looked at the ceiling
My laddies said he I loved the salt sea, in the days when the trawls I
    was haulin'
This life on the sea was Heaven to me, when I fished on Harbour Grace
    Island.

We had the Snows and the Ashes you know, the Martins and Noels I
    remember
We all got our share when the fish they were there, and we finished our
    voyage in November
The women were there with the combs in their hair, and they kept all
    the family smilin'
In the morning the smoke would sure make you choke, when we fished
    on Harbour Grace Island.

Oh God bless the days and the old fashioned ways, when the people
    were so kind and hearty
And most every night it sure was a sight, when we went to a ball or a
    party
Then came the spring and the robins did sing, our traps and our trawls
    we were coilin'

With a good southwest breeze we sailed o'er the sea, to fish on Harbour
     Grace Island.

As Grandfather rocked in his old rocking chair, his memory related
     the story
He spoke of the place in his own Harbour Grace, with its history of
     fame and great glory
And that old tan pot it sure smelled a lot, whenever it came to a boilin'
But I tell you my friend I would do it again, fish out there on Harbour
     Grace Island.

In the days long gone by we had sorrow and joy, and our sea boots were
     all made of leather
It sure is no bluff our boats were real tough, and could stand up in big
     stormy weather
The women you know wore all calico, their dresses were long but still
     stylin'
No one ever did see a fair lady's knee, when we fished on Harbour
     Grace Island.

The women worked hard with the gardens and flakes, and also helped
     out in the stages
What a story is told of those fair ladies bold, it takes up a good many
     pages
They were there from the start and they sure did their part, climbing
     the cliffs without fallin'
They wore button shoes and cooked fish and brewis, when they lived
     on Harbour Grace Island.

Gone are the days and the old fishing ways, which will live both in song
     and in story
Of the times now gone by with its sorrow and joy, surrounded by history
     and glory
The Island today still lies in the Bay, but no more are the fishing bells
     tollin'

May the Heaven above send down its love, on the people of Harbour
  Grace Island.

Written by Gordon Snow inspired by a poem by Captain Jack Dodd.

GLOSSARY

banking schooners. Vessels once used to carry fishermen to the fishing grounds. Arriving there, the men were lowered over the side in smaller boats called dories from which they conducted fishing operations. The dories returned to the schooner at the end of each day with their catch that was then processed into salted fish and stored in the fish hold.

caboose. An iron pot used in the boat to contain a fire for boiling water and heating food.

canker. A disease in the form of a growth found on potatoes.

cod trap. A box-type net used to catch cod.

culler. A person who inspects fish and determines the grade on which payment is based.

dray. A cart with two large wheels pulled by a horse and used to haul cargo.

duff. A pudding made with flour and flavoured with blueberries, raisins, or molasses.

fathom. Length or depth measurement of six feet.

fish and brewis. A meal made by boiling salted fish and hard bread that has been soaked overnight in water; scrunchions (fried pieces of pork fat) are spread over it for flavour.

gaff. A short pole with a hook on one end primarily used to haul fish in over the side of the boat.

gannet. A marine bird noted for diving from great heights into the sea to catch fish.

grapnel. A small anchor.

gunnel. The top part of the sides of a boat.

hand-lining. A method of fishing using a single line, a lead sinker and a baited hook that is dropped over the side of the boat and held in the hand.

jiggs' dinner. A meal prepared by cooking vegetables together in a pot and flavoured with salt beef or pork.

killick. A homemade anchor that has four arms of wood. The stock is made from four long sticks attached to the arms and tied at the top and holds a rectangular beach rock for ballast.

'lassy. A common name for molasses; hence, 'lassy buns, 'lassy bread, etc.

longers. Long sticks of wood, usually fir or spruce, used to build fences, flakes, etc.

mauzy day. A day with light rain and sometimes fog and very little wind.

mug-up. A light lunch, especially before retiring.

oilskins. A jacket, pants, and hat combination worn by fishermen that repels water.

pickets. Small fir or spruce sticks used for fencing.

pooks. Piles of dry hay.

quintal. A unit of measurement; usually 112 pounds.

rounders. Small, eviscerated codfish that have been salted and dried.

sounds. The air bladders of cod that are preserved by salting.

splits. Small lengths of wood that have been cut with an axe into smaller lengthwise pieces and used to light fires; a form of kindling.

stage. A facility built near the water's edge used as premises for conducting fishing operations.

stage-head. A crude wharf extending from the stage out over the water to permit the unloading of fish from the boat.

THOMAS SNOW

Thomas Snow was born in Harbour Grace in 1908 to Thomas and Julia-Ann Snow. His early life was typical of those families associated with fishing at the time, and he was an integral part of his family fishing enterprise. In order to obtain his own spending money, he took the job of delivering the weekly newspaper, *Harbour Grace Standard*, at age twelve with one cent received for each one sold, but the paper cost only two cents. A short while later, he delivered groceries after school and on Saturdays for a local grocer, W.H. Parmiter. In winter, his dog Sport would help him with the deliveries by hauling the sled. Late in his fourteenth year he left school and worked for three dollars per month in Martin Sheppard's retail store. Education was not forgotten however, because he used two dollars of that money to pay his fee to his teacher Mr. John Davis for night school each month,

Endeavouring to improve his income away from fishing, Thomas became employed at Archibald's Shoe Factory in 1926 at age eighteen for a salary of $3.50 per week. When that factory closed in 1932, he returned to the fishery for two years before finding employment in another local shoe factory owned by F. W. McKay & Son, as foreman. In 1945 he became manager and worked there until it closed in 1949.

After a short stint with the federal government he became employed as a supervisor in the Boys' Home and Training School on Bell Island, but was transferred to Whitbourne in 1953. He still maintained residence in Harbour Grace. In 1954 he took employment in his hometown as foreman in the new shoe factory, Koch Shoes Limited, and was manager there from 1958 until its closure in 1971. From 1972 to his retirement in 1985, he owned and operated a small convenience store business.

Married to Florence Sheppard in 1951, they had five daughters, Marjorie, Cecily, Gloria, Judy, Susan and four sons Tom, Peter, Steven, and Bob.

Thomas received the Governor General's Fire Service Exemplary Service Medal for forty years of service in the Harbour Grace Volunteer Fire Brigade and was also a Life Member of the Brigade. The Harbour Grace Regatta Committee made him a life member and he was inducted as a member of the Harbour Grace Sports Hall of Fame as an athlete/builder. He was also active in other fraternal and civic organizations in the town.

Thomas was the last survivor of the family of Thomas and Julia-Ann Snow as described in this book. Two of his stepbrothers, George and Albert, died in the Boston area and another, William, passed away a number of years after returning from the United States. Brothers Robert and Walter and two sisters, Lillian and Bessie, all lived in Harbour Grace and passed away there.

Book Two

SURVIVAL OF SALMO

Gordon Snow

To all those who spend freely of their time in the conservation of Atlantic salmon and the recreational anglers who partake in this fabulous sport.

Living with Nature

We live in an environmentally conscious world
And we have to find our own niche,
To become part of an ecosystem
Whether we are poor or rich.
We are an organism of nature
Propagating our biotic life,
Protecting our food chain and habitat,
For natural selection means strife.

There's one thing we may not realize
When we cause pollution each day,
What about other creatures of nature
In the pyramid of life, shall we say?
If we protect our environment
And give animals a chance to survive,
It will help us to live right with nature
And keep our own species alive.

Gordon Snow
American Poetry Anthology, 1990

ACKNOWLEDGEMENTS

Special thanks to Judy Beveridge in retyping the contents of this book for the revision, and also to the Atlantic Salmon Federation and the Atlantic Salmon Trust for the images used.

INTRODUCTION

Atlantic salmon are an anadromous species which means they are born in fresh water, migrate to the marine environment, but return to the rivers of their birth to spawn. Spawning occurs in the fall but the young are not hatched until the following spring and are known as 'alevins.' Salmon spend two to four years in fresh water during which time they are generally referred to as 'parr.' On their final year in fresh water they assume a silvery appearance and are known as 'smolt.'

Atlantic salmon are very widespread and range from New England to Greenland in the western Atlantic and from Portugal to Russia in the eastern Atlantic.

High-seas fisheries for salmon make management difficult. Countries producing salmon in their rivers have no control over them when they enter the marine environment and undertake extensive migration patterns. International agreements have been established for Atlantic salmon to help manage the commercial fisheries. Regulations have been established to curb both commercial and recreational fisheries.

Pollution has helped to reduce the number of salmon in coastal and fresh waters. Migrating salmon often come in contact with polluted water as they approach their rivers before ascending to spawn. Larger rivers especially are also linked to chemical pollutants from industry that often dot the shorelines.

Respect for the environment is gradually gaining more prominence among the general public. Stricter regulations are being promulgated to deal with polluters. A conscious change is taking place among the general public and more regard is given to environmental issues.

However, a more insidious issue is the discharge of pharmaceuticals including drugs of all kinds, insecticides, and pesticides that eventually find their way into freshwater environments. The long-term effects take considerable time to determine because of the large number of these pollutants and the time it takes to discover cause and effect.

There have been success stories of fish returning to areas of restored habitat during the past few years. The return of fish is a good indicator of improvement in water quality. Salmon is a very hardy species and can survive a number of challenges, including many forms of pollution. However, even though salmon may appear to be doing well, we sometimes don't know the effects of even mild chemicals on their ability to complete their normal life cycle.

Much salmon habitat has been destroyed through commercial development. Towns and cities have been built on the shores of major rivers and industrial development associated with them has taken its toll. The building of dams has disrupted salmon migration, but in many cases fish ladders have been incorporated into dam sites to allow migration to continue. Most projects now have to go through an environmental assessment before they can proceed, if at all.

There have been cantankerous vibes between commercial fishermen and recreational anglers in relation to conservation. Recreational fishermen blame commercial fishing for destroying salmon before they can ascend the rivers to spawn. Commercial fishermen blame the recreational fishermen for catching them while they are preparing to spawn in the rivers. In actuality, good conservation lies somewhere in between. Regulations have been applied to both types of fisheries, but poaching among recreational and commercial fishermen exist. Coupled with that is the incidental catches of the species while fishing for other fish stocks. No amount of enforcement by regulatory agencies is enough to ensure propagation of salmon and other similar species and the collective good-will of all concerned is required.

One alternative is to combine forces of wildlife and other regulatory officers to provide more 'eyes and ears' for patrols, coupled with new surveillance technology. Prevention is the best alternative and many conservation-minded citizens are now reporting poachers. Courts are dealing harshly with convicted persons and that acts as a further deterrent to would-be poachers.

***

Atlantic salmon are considered to be the 'king of fishes.' Recreational fishing for Atlantic salmon is a great sport practised for centuries by Europeans and North Americans. Aboriginals have been taking salmon for centuries as part of their annual food supply. Many rivers that once had populations of salmon are devoid of them. However, more emphasis is now being placed on returning the rivers to the salmon. Many conservation and public interest groups are joining forces to clean up the environment. Salmon are being reintroduced to rivers that previously had populations, but through overfishing, poaching, and pollution their numbers have been greatly reduced.

Salmon fishing is an excellent leisure-time activity. The challenges given to the angler in trying to catch a salmon have been described many times as humans match wits with fish and often losing. Anglers spend hours and hours casting over the pools in the hope of enticing a salmon to take the fly and let the battle begin. Patience is one virtue an angler must have in order to be successful. Salmon angling is really a duel of patience.

What is the long-term outlook for Atlantic salmon? The rapidly growing aquaculture industry for salmon in the north Atlantic is providing plenty of salmon for commercial distribution. However, recreational salmon fishing continues to be a popular activity and many rivers are now more accessible.

There is a strong lobby by conservationists including recreational salmon fishermen to reduce and eliminate all commercial fishing and this has mainly happened. With populations of wild Atlantic salmon showing signs of declining stocks in most areas, efforts are now more employed to rebuilding salmon stocks as the main emphasis. However, because salmon spend part of their life cycle in marine waters, often far from their birthplace, international conservation is required to maintain and increase abundance and such co-operation is often not easy to obtain. There are still countries that have a commercial salmon fishery.

Let's hope the trials and tribulations of Salmo as told in the following pages of this book may foster more salmon conservation in the years ahead. It is mainly through the work of organizations like the Salmon Protection Association for the Waters of Newfoundland (SPAWN), Salmon Association of Eastern Newfoundland (SAEN), Atlantic Salmon Federation (ASF), the Atlantic Salmon Trust (AST) and the North Atlantic Salmon Conservation Organization (NASCO) that will enable all concerned to ensure salmon populations are maintained and increased for future generations.

In the original version of this book I stated, "It is hoped the perseverance displayed by Salmo will encourage more people to become conservation-minded and help those now involved to continue their efforts toward increasing the abundance of Atlantic salmon." Over twenty years later, it is still appropriate.

CHAPTER ONE

GENESIS OF SALMO

My name is Salmo. I was born in a redd (the depression made in the river bottom by the female salmon in which to lay her eggs for fertilization by the male) about fourteen miles upstream on Long Harbour River, Fortune Bay, in the Province of Newfoundland and Labrador, Canada. The exact day was March 28, several years after Canada proclaimed her two-hundred-mile limit. Yes, I am a proud Canadian from Canada's newest province, ready to initiate my journey in life that is full of intrigue and sometimes considered mysterious. I am another of the species of Atlantic salmon that for millennia have been born in northern rivers and managed to maintain and manifest existence to the present day, albeit with some difficulty after *Homo sapiens* came on the scene.

It is a cool, clear day as I emerge from my egg with the yolk sac still intact to provide nourishment during the early stages of my life. This is necessary because unlike humans, salmon have to fend for themselves from birth with no parental care. I know this is precarious and is the reason why my mother produced so many eggs. If my mother were to lay only one egg, our existence would probably be short-lived. Since there are hundreds of eggs laid, we have a chance at least to survive the various types of devastation that may befall us, like ice, silt, predation, uncomfortable water temperatures, and river-bed disturbances. If I had parental care like you do, my infancy and adolescence would be more positive, but I'm left to perform my own postnatal functions. However, no use complaining. I will try to live life to the fullest.

As I circumnavigate my hatching area day after day with brothers and sisters, the daylight hours become longer and my yolk sac smaller. In about a month my yolk sac disappears, depriving me of ready nutrients, but I am now free swimming and ready to leave my birthing area. I have by now learned to feed and my digestive and excretory systems are fully functional. Small organisms are in good supply, and as I continue to forage my weight increases slowly.

Days become weeks, weeks become months and then years, bringing changes in my colours and sometimes my demeanour. Black spots develop on my sides like bars. I have ten, but others may have from nine to thirteen plus a few red spots too, just to make me a little more handsome and more aggressive. Oh yes, it is during this colourful stage I am known as a "parr."

I can drag my story to the limit describing all my narrow escapes during the next few river years. Nature is often tough on me while I'm trying to shelter from those large pieces of ice during spring breakups. Sometimes that stuff gets caught in the river and causes a buildup that crowds our territory. Luckily the rocks help to divert the ice away from our many hiding places. Those rocks you see in rivers and streams are really multipurpose in regard to the safety and well-being of our species. They provide shelter from swiftly flowing water and floating ice and deflect the water while helping to oxygenate it. When you see rapids or a falls in a river, you are looking at oxygenation in action.

Broken trees too often give us a fright as they float downstream. However, when they get stuck along the way, they offer shelter and shade us, especially from the hot sun. Sometimes overhanging branches of trees provide us with shady areas and keep us safer because we are not so readily observed in the shadows. At one time the harvesting of trees was often detrimental to us salmon because logs were driven down many rivers as a means of getting them to shipping ports or paper mills. Luckily, that practice has been curtailed or even stopped.

Then there are the human atrocities against us, such as the use of all-terrain vehicles that traverse our river shorelines to stir up silt and that disturbs the riverbed. So if you do come in close proximity to a river or stream, remember that young salmon may be living there. Please respect our habitat.

We sometimes have to be careful of those pesky mergansers too, the scourge of the duck family as far as I'm concerned. They just stand there, watching for their chance, and as soon as one of us unknowingly leaves himself or herself open, just one dip of the beak and the merganser puts on weight.

Need I remind you, I am not the only salmon in the river. There are hundreds of us and a few young trout as well. I will have to remain active to survive among this lot. There are days when I wish God were around to pull off that miracle again just to get rid of a few of us. You know the one about the five barley loaves and two small fishes, as long as He wouldn't select me, of course. After all, we have to protect our own self-interest.

Prowling along on the bottom of our habitat is another creature that I particularly like to give plenty of space. They have an opposite migration compared to us and travel to the Sargasso Sea south of Bermuda and east of the Bahamas in the Atlantic Ocean to spawn. I am referring to eels that have the scientific names *Anguilla rostrata* (American eel) or *Anguilla Anguilla* (European eel.) They are carnivorous with sharp teeth and will eat almost everything they think will be a food item. That includes us salmon, but gladly they spend most of their time on muddy bottoms while we prefer gravelly areas. Apart from some of the larger birds, eels have few enemies while in fresh water. Sadly, they spend many years in fresh water, but every year a number of them leave and head south to spawn and presumably die.

There is one experience I will tell you about if you will permit. It concerns the occasion when a young lad hooked me on an artificial fly, and I flew through the air with the grace of a pelican. Lucky for me the lad's father was nearby. When he saw me, he explained to his son that what he had caught is a young salmon and it has to be released. I can tell you, Salmo was never happier. The boy wet his hands, disengaged me from the hook and gracefully returned me to the water. A lesson for both of us. I wish all stories concerning the catching of parr would end like this, and many do.

SALMONOIDS

The metamorphosis of Salmo from parr to smolt as he prepares to leave Long Harbour River. Note the gradual loss of the black bars and the development of dorsal black spots and silvery ventral area. (Atlantic Salmon Trust)

The parr stage is a relatively slow growth period. But if you had to compete among a bunch of young salmon and trout, you might not grow very fast either. Nevertheless, the high waters in the rivers experienced during the spring resulting from the melting snow and the effect of ice all contribute to provide food for us finfishes. I am lucky because I can forage for myself on various insects. I am known to be slightly carnivorous on occasion, but I don't brag about that for obvious reasons. By the way, did you realize that plants can live without animals, but animals can't live without plants? Many of you humans have become regimented to a vegetarian or vegan diet that relates to eating plants only. For those people, that big juicy steak, marinated and cooked to perfection and smothered in caramelized onions has no appeal. Cattle are all vegetarian, so I suppose you meat eaters feel that you too, are vegetarians, even though it is an indirect acquisition of plants.

So to return to my story, there is a reason for all those eggs. Mother Nature knows what is best and appropriate. You must remember too, that our mothers might die after they lay their eggs. The rigours of reaching the spawning beds and the stress of egg-laying sometimes take its toll. Of course I think that my mother is still living. Any female that can produce an offspring as hardy as I am certainly can withstand spawning. Why not say so? I'm not bashful.

Life here during my first few years is rather pleasant, playing with my friends and scattering from enemies. My growth continues to be as good as the rest of my progeny, and by my fourth birthday I am thirteen centimetres in length, which for you non-metrified people is about five inches.

I find I can now catch certain items of food that often escaped me previously. My attack mechanisms have improved, and I am becoming more predator than prey. Juicy morsels on the river bottom such as dragonfly larvae are now part of my diet. Flying insects that land on the water are often easy prey for me.

The parr stage of Atlantic salmon while living in fresh water. (Atlantic Salmon Trust)

We fish of course don't bother to chew everything. It is just gulped down into our stomachs and allowed to gradually digest. Now we do use our teeth for holding prey and for cutting off pieces of food from a larger piece. Sometimes I even bite off more than I can chew, but we all do that on occasion.

As fishes in the river, we don't have to make any extra effort to use the bathroom. We simply take care of everything here in the river and the flow of the water washes feces downstream as it dissipates. It is a veritable sewage system provided by nature itself. Not only that, but the wastage from our bodies ends up as food for bottom-living creatures or becomes part of the nutrients on the bottom that supports flora like eel grasses to maintain our habitat. The river ecosystem works well and is continually in operation.

A phenomenon soon occurs. Here I am one day with little bars along my sides when suddenly I begin to turn all silver as the black gradually disappears. I pay no attention to it, because after all, my mother and father were silver so it would not be strange if I mirrored their beauty, well their image anyway.

The winter ice melts as the days pass and I get the urge to head downstream, leaving the relative safety of my childhood habitat. The same happens to my companions, but I'm not sure who decides to head downstream first.

In any event, off we go at about the same age human children begin pre-kindergarten. What a real coincidence. Even though I have to fend for myself, the learning curve experienced in my river has taught many lessons that enable me to grow and develop.

I may be presumptuous, but it is after the acquisition of my silvery state that I am now a smolt. Why I turn this silvery colour is not readily apparent here in the river, but may become obvious later.

The journey downstream is relatively easy because we are going with the flow. Down we go through Ten Mile Pool, Seven Mile Pool, and on to Mitchell's Pool near the mouth of Long Harbour River and finally into brackish water.

Certainly is more space out here and the water is quite different. I notice a pronounced salinity as I wander around the lower reaches of my river on the high tide. I can feel the resistance of the current as the water from the river enters the sea and meets the incoming tide. There is more food here than you can shake a stick at, so to speak. Whoopee! These little critters are all so filling. Stand back you watchers of weight!

My body soon adjusts to the salt water and it appears that I have more buoyancy which makes it easier for me to swim. My body's transition from fresh to salt water is really a good adaptation as I continue to gorge myself on the copious amounts of waterborne food. Here where the river meets the sea, an upwelling occurs that congregates food particles in suspension and that makes it easier for me eat at my leisure.

Very soon a passion for further adventure overtakes me, a sort of longing to get out and fulfill some predestined goal in life. On the next high tide out through Long Harbour itself I go, along with some others, seeking adventure and trusting I will know how to cope.

During my stay in brackish water food was plentiful, and my physical condition improved. Out here in Fortune Bay the supply is even better. It is believed all life evolved from the sea and I'm beginning to feel at home already. I need more food now because of the extra swimming that requires more energy output.

Where will this cruise take me? Why am I doing it? What is driving me out to sea? How do I know I will find my way back? I wish I had a compass, direction finder, or satellite navigation like navigators have on board their vessels. Oh, but I have an inherited GPS built in, just like you have in some of your vehicles! All of our salmon species are born with it. You could say we are fully equipped.

The next thing I realize is we are swimming past the French Islands of St. Pierre and Miquelon. I bet the French don't even know we are here. Of course neither do the Canadians. National waters mean little to us because we use them all. Lines on a map have little effect on our swimming habits. One minute we are French fish, the next minute Canadian fish. I didn't notice any difference between swimming on the French side of the economic zone and swimming on the Canadian side. However, since I was born in Canada, I suppose I am Canadian, but I do have free access into French waters and no requirement for a visa. Anyway, *au revoir.*

Imagine, Salmo out in the middle of Fortune Bay without a compass! I am not alone and all my buddies appear to know where they are going.

Who's leading whom is difficult to establish. The sun, moon, and stars can affect direction, but temperature and currents may also be involved. In any event, this marine cruise has begun. Next we speed across the mouth of Placentia Bay, around the south-eastern tip of the Island of Newfoundland at Cape Race and 'hard-to-port.' We all scurry in the same general direction, slowing down only for occasional food and rest. The trip north closely follows the receding ice, and food is more abundant there. I suppose it has something to do with the Labrador Current flowing from the north and the Gulf Stream bringing warmer water from the south, both converging and providing up-wellings that usually mean abundant food supplies. Whatever it is, I feel delighted, at least gastronomically.

I wonder why I head north. Maybe it goes back to my origins. Theory has it that all salmon previously lived in the northern seas, and the Ice Age was responsible for bringing us farther south. Therefore, this would explain the inherent tendency to swim north. There must be some answer to it because I am on my way without any discernible reason. I just know this is the proper direction and I am programmed to proceed toward higher latitudes.

CHAPTER TWO

MARINE JOURNEY

As the days and months pass, I continue to put on weight and my capacity to capture larger prey increases. But as I get bigger and better looking, I see larger predators eyeing me hungrily. If there is such a thing as safety in numbers, I'm safe here among my companions. Nevertheless, a few of our number have fallen prey to the seals that are all around us. Those creatures can't move very fast on land, but in the water they can strike quickly. My strength and speed have allowed me to outlast all my predators, up to this point at least.

I not only have to deal with seals but fishing nets as well. I can escape the nets because the mesh size in most of them permits me to pass through. However, this will not be possible much longer, and I have to be careful, especially when chasing prey.

The use of nets for catching fish has been practised for many centuries. Fishing nets are usually restricted by mesh size, but it depends on the species being harvested. If they are fishing herring, the mesh size is small, but if fishing for turbot, the mesh size is much larger. Therefore, in my initial time at sea I have to be wary of smaller-mesh nets, but when I get bigger, the larger-mesh nets will become a problem. Sometimes salmon can become entangled in nets regardless of the mesh size. A salmon like me has to have keen eyesight to steer away from nets, and that's not easy when those hard-to-see monofilament nets are being used. Fishers use those nets because they are more effective by being difficult to see and they are more durable because they exhibit very little biodegradability. Many of those nets become lost for various reasons and are found on the bottoms of oceans, sometimes still trapping unwary fish species.

Nets are a very efficient method of catching fish. Their use goes back to biblical times when Peter cast his nets. They are used to trap all kinds of fish by entrapping them in schools or by meshing them by the gills. They come in many forms and some are active while others are passive. Nets can entrap fish such as us salmon by surrounding us or lying in wait on the surface in a stationary fashion. The most prolific but yet destructive of the nets are drift nets. These are nets many miles long set out on the high seas and they catch whatever happens to come along. It could be seals, whales, seabirds, dolphins, turtles, many kinds of pelagic fish, and yes even salmon. I'm glad you humans are finally realizing the damage such nets can cause and are stopping their use for the sake of marine conservation. Drift nets really amount to overkill and are non-selective.

Anyway that's enough morbid discussion, because here I am with the big Atlantic Ocean as my playground. Now that I stop to consider, it must appear strange that salmon don't head south like humans. Many of you fly off to Florida, or some other warm place in the winter and early spring, and I make a beeline for the Labrador Sea. I suppose we prefer the cooler waters and let our catadromous friends, the eels, have the Sargasso Sea to themselves. I'm not sure I would want to be there with them anyway. As you already know, they do prey on us sometimes when we are in the river together during our early years.

While I'm on the subject, my life would be miserable in the south. There would be larger fish to chase me as well as those long-mouthed, reptile creatures, the alligators. I would be gobbled up in jig time. My ancestors made the right decision, so I will take my chances with the seals and the toothed whales. I can outswim them anyway, unless I get ambushed, but that's not easy with my dexterity.

The cold Labrador Current, the warmer Greenland Current, and subsequent up-wellings all have an effect on our food supply. I am already approaching one kilogram. In fact our whole salmon school is doing fine on the growth ledger. As I grow I require more food, but my muscles are stronger which improves propulsion through the water to catch more prey. I am a magnificent specimen of beauty, strength, agility, and modesty. I see salmon out here over ten kilograms, but generally speaking, most of us are below five kilograms.

I understand there were more large salmon in past years, but of course there were more salmon of all sizes. Rivers that previously had good salmon populations are now the homes for relatively small numbers and a number of rivers are devoid of salmon altogether.

Why is my species in continuous decline? Then again, so are many other species.

I can give some of the reasons as passed down from my ancestors and from my own limited knowledge. They include aerial spraying that affected our habitat and food supply; disruption of habitat through for instance, siltation or even elimination of spawning areas; freshwater predators such as mergansers, gulls, and eels; industrial activities that caused destruction of habitat through pollution and man-made (have to be careful using that term because some of my female swimming companions are touchy about it) obstructions; wanton logging and sawmill practices that deprived us of river habitat; heavy angling and commercial fishing pressure; and poaching, the complete disregard for our species and the law. Many of us have been taken accidentally by fishers fishing for other species, and that is referred to as by-catch. The problems are as varied as the solutions.

There has been eloquent argument over one particular conservation measure and its effect over time on the decrease in size generally of Atlantic salmon populations. I refer to the mesh size of the nets. When commercial fishing for salmon was ongoing, there was a minimum mesh size for nets, which in effect, allowed small salmon to escape by passing through the mesh. However, this meant that all salmon subsequently taken were larger. If for over twenty to thirty years you continually take the large salmon, wouldn't this lead to a proliferation of small salmon or grilse? Many of these small salmon spend only one year at sea before returning to the river to spawn, and the number of eggs laid would be far less than the number laid by larger salmon.

Genetically, those one-sea-winter salmon produce offspring that would carry the same traits. Therefore, wouldn't we end up with all small salmon that are generally referred to as fish weighing approximately two kilos or less? Just a thought. The numbers of larger salmon are decreasing and I have not seen many over five kilos. Of course that is only an observation on my part.

Daylight hours are decreasing here just south of the midnight sun. The winter solstice gradually prepares us, as has happened for longer than my ancestors can remember. The skies take on a more sombre look, and the water becomes heavier as it cools, not that it was very warm before. Flocks of birds are heading south to escape the onset of winter. It is amazing how desolate the north can be in the winter, yet in summer become the breeding, nursing, and feeding grounds for so many creatures.

As the birds have migrated to safety, I begin moving south along the coastal edges of the Labrador Sea, but not too close to land. Since I live underwater, I am not subjected to the same extremes as animals that have to adjust to ambient temperatures. Therefore, there is no need for me to travel very far south. The temperature of the water does have an effect on me. We are what are referred to as "cold-blooded" animals or, as scientists call us, exothermal. This means that our body temperatures are controlled by the temperature around us. Maybe this explains why we show up at different places at different times of the year and our appearance each year may not be the same for many localities. We seek water temperatures suitable for us, and since tides and currents in the oceans are subject to change, our migration routes may also change.

During periods of cooler water temperatures, we tend to slow down. This is both good and bad. Good in the sense we conserve energy because we have slowed down, but bad in the sense we have to be on guard for faster predators. It all works out because if we are slowed down, so are the others, except for marine mammals that are warm-blooded and maintain their own body temperatures.

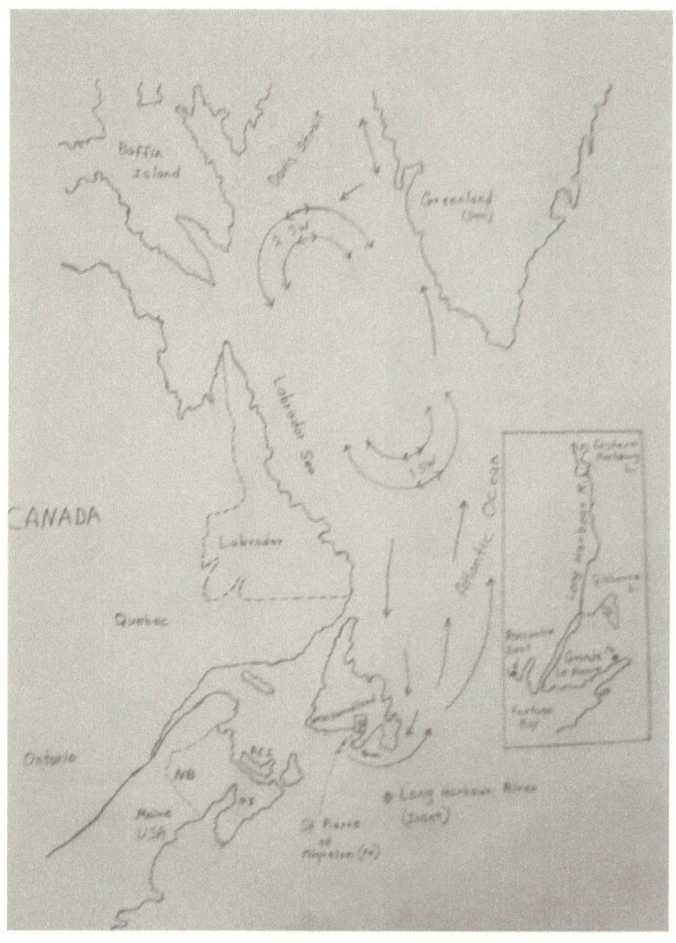

**The migration route of Salmo when he spent two years
at sea in the marine environment. (G. Snow)**

CHAPTER THREE

SEASONAL DIFFERENCES AT SEA

Winter approaches and finally the North Atlantic succumbs to ice conditions, colder temperatures and far less daylight. I cruise around along the edge of the ice, feeding as I go. Seals appear in search of food in large numbers on occasion, as the females prepare for their most celebrated births on the icefields in March.

I'm sure you have all heard about the harp seals that occupy the northern environs in large numbers. There are millions of these seal critters around, and they really move in the water. It is one creature that breathes air yet is entirely at home in the water. They don't have legs for land use, but flippers for paddling in the water. They can enjoy both the land and sea environments and are living on the edge of both ways of life, but are neither pure land nor pure sea animals. I don't want to spend too much time talking about seals, but they have caused some worldwide controversy. As far as I'm concerned, I wish they would evolve feet and stay on the land and the ice.

The passing of winter finds me approaching the southern edge of my migration path. I have survived my first winter at sea. The changes of spring bring increasing daylight and the whole ocean seems to be taking on a new vitality. I see huge masses of cod congregating to undertake their spawning ritual on the high seas.

Every now and again I see a large net-contraption fall to the bottom of the ocean and move along for a while, only to disappear again as it is retrieved. You people refer to this as 'otter- trawling,' which has become the dominant means of catching many species, including cod and shrimp. I can just lounge around of course and watch all the action, making sure I give those otter-trawl nets plenty of room. Since I swim mainly in the upper column of water, the otter trawls riding along the seabed do not cause me any concern.

As spawning cod perform their propagating tasks, millions of eggs begin floating around, each one a potential new codfish. Of course, they all don't hatch because they are preyed on by many creatures. Those eggs float to the surface for up to fifty days before hatching. They taste good, too. Oops, now I have told you. It's a good thing codfish lay millions of eggs.

Summer brings many forms of added nourishment as the tiny eggs of various fish species hatch in abundance. Tides and currents do their work in circulating food around the oceans, and up-wellings provide a proliferation of nutrients. Just as blood moves nutrients around the body, the ocean currents move nutrients around ocean bodies. Anyway after coming through the winter, I'm ready for the robust period of summer.

I just can't seem to get everything perfect. Just as weather and water conditions improve, summer brings with it the usual share of migratory predators, including the species commonly referred to as jaws. Since we often navigate in the upper two or three fathoms of the Atlantic Ocean, we can be easily detected by larger predators such as sharks and toothed whales that occupy the same ocean strata on many occasions. Even though the ocean is large, wherever abundant food fish are found the predators somehow have the ability to find them. The food chains of life are vibrant systems and form part of a more complex food web of which I am only one small entity.

Take for instance krill, those tiny crustaceans found prolifically in the Antarctic.

The krill are like the blood that we have circulating in our bodies. They are carried around by the currents, providing nourishment for many marine creatures as they go. Some people consider krill the ultimate form of energy and they are at the bottom of the marine food pyramid. Humans have also become predators of krill because this species is now being harvested for the production of krill oil, a major component of which is Omega-3. Salmon also have valuable fish oil containing Omega-3, but for obvious reasons I won't dwell on it for too long.

There is apprehension about the fishery based on krill, but scientists and others agree that commercial harvesting can be sustained with the current knowledge of abundance. You know from experience that it is very difficult to count larger finfish and forecast abundance levels. Therefore, I doubt whether humans can count krill and establish meaningful abundance indices.

That is the amazing thing about the study of animals. In my case, you have spent millions trying to find out more about me. You know about my spawning habits, migratory patterns to a certain extent, and a little about my eating habits. You still don't know how I return to the same river of my birth to spawn. Well, I'm going to tell you. Where else would I go? It is better to go to a place I already know than some strange place. You humans know that after each working day married persons return to the homes of the people they love. Yes, I am aware there are occasions when you go other places. In my particular case, I believe one of those girls I grew up with will be with me in our own river when the time comes.

How did I get sidetracked when I was talking about food? Well, anything I suppose to pass away the few last days of summer.

Once again, the phenomenon of fall brings with it changes relevant to the time, and my voracious eating during the summer has left me plump as pie. Things begin slowing down again, and I become less agile. I have extended myself farther north, taking advantage of Danas, Fiskaenas, and Hellefiske banks off the coast of Greenland. Here again the fishermen become our prime enemy as they capitalize on the short season. By October I am saying farewell to the Godthaab area and heading southwest into the Labrador Sea to spend the winter.

They say the submarines found us salmon along the edges of the ice off Greenland. This prompted a fishery that did not help our numbers at all. We used this area as sort of a meeting of the clans, because salmon showed up here from all over eastern North America. It must be related to some ancestral ties and even though we don't wear kilts or tartans, we do sport a pleasant, silvery sheen.

The discovery of our northern migration prompted international discussions among producing countries that have spent time and financial resources supporting rivers where we spawn. If these countries were doing everything possible to produce salmon, it would be wasted if the fishery adjacent to Greenland were not curbed. There has to be co-operation among many nations if you are to keep us maintained. We need protection for all phases of our life cycle.

Preparing for my second winter at sea is not as difficult. I am heavier and stronger and compete successfully for food with my companions. Generally speaking, my life in this marine environment is also becoming routinely enjoyable. Apart from my natural predators and fishing activities, the difference in weather above the water has little effect on me. I am sometimes influenced by water temperatures, but can move to favourable zones very quickly. This can necessitate changes in migration patterns that affect food supply. However, prey also seek temperatures close to mine which is very convenient. You already know I can survive in fresh or salt water, so any differences I encounter in salinity do not affect me or my comrades.

Sometimes though, we get caught offshore because of colder water temperatures near land, but our bodies are capable of seeking out the proper temperatures for sustaining life. This is a natural adaptation to keep us from getting trapped in water areas that have unfavourable water conditions. While we can withstand ranges in water temperatures, we try to stay within our preferred environmental range as much as possible.

CHAPTER FOUR

YEARNING TO HEAD HOME

The solitude of winter passes and I detect fundamental movement again as if drawn by some unknown force. Something strange and unexplained is taking over my body and I am precipitating the start of a voyage, a return voyage. Yes, I have the urge to start a long journey and the desire to go home.

My body is undergoing general changes and endocrine secretions signal a purposeful move south, but not just a simple movement to obtain food. It is a more dedicated action to abolish my marine environment. This is something I cannot explain but is inherent in my species.

I begin to eat more voraciously now, as if I have to hurry before all the food is gone. Every ounce of strength that I have is garnered for the trip ahead and I am not the only one affected. Many in our school are encountering the same type of body seizure. An instinct of some kind is autonomously telling us what to do. An inexplicable homing device is taking charge much the same as if I have an urge to do a particular thing and can't stop myself. Everything else now becomes secondary.

As spring draws to a close, I am just north of the Funk Islands off Newfoundland. Never have I seen so much food! Millions of capelin are congregated for the spawning invasion of the beaches that historically begins in the middle to latter part of June, but is happening later in recent years.

Capelin travel in large masses, a common procedure among small pelagic species. Even so, they all appear to know where they are going, but how they all turn in the same direction at once is remarkable. The male capelin is easily distinguishable from the female by the spawning ridges along its sides. I'm not certain what these ridges have to do with the, pardon the expression, sex act. Perhaps this ridge sensitizes the female as the male rubs close to her seeking mutual intent. However, I'm only fantasizing now because I don't have spawning ridges.

Scientists say there are capelin that spawn on the Grand Banks rather than make the trip to land to perform this ritual. Why some capelin spawn offshore while others go to the shoreline to spawn is unknown. Perhaps the capelin that spawn on the Grand Banks actually come from somewhere else. Was the Grand Banks above sea level at one time? If it was then that could explain it. In any event, I am glad they are here to increase our predator-prey relationship. Capelin are an important prey for many predators, including larger fish, mammals, and birds.

The drift ice is certainly extensive, hugging the coastline with the influence of onshore winds. The effect of ice on the normal habits of fish and marine mammals is complex. Fishermen are often influenced by drifting ice that delays the start of their fishing season. There have been years when fishermen were delayed in their fishing operations until late May or June around Newfoundland. You could say ice is Nature's way to conserve us salmon as well as other species. However, fishermen are not so happy about it.

As I proceed farther south, the icebergs become sparser and the drift ice gives way to open water along the coastline. The ice will retreat fast as temperatures move higher. How majestic those icebergs are, shining brilliantly as the sun beats down on them sometimes causing colourful images. Rivulets of flowing water within the bergs gradually weaken them until parts break off and when this happens it is said that the iceberg is 'calving.' I'm not sure the name fits because icebergs certainly don't appear to look much like cows.

It's been very smooth sailing so far in the upper surface of the ocean as the large ice cubes continue to disappear and the water temperature rises. Not that it's too warm out here, but I relish the gradual warmth.

It is gratifying to have an abundant supply of food as we accompany the capelin to land. This permits us to obtain adequate food supplies without spending too much energy. The capelin know where they are going, too. Just as they dissipate into seemingly smaller groups, we also divide into distinct schools as land draws near.

I hit land near Cape Bonavista, just as John Cabot did, and head south along with many others. Capelin are presumably waiting for the right biological time before striking land. Sexual maturity for many must be later, but most of the males are now showing their corresponding spawning ridges. Judging by their appearance, some of them will be spawning into late July.

A number of my female companions are looking better to me every day with their bright scales, white tummies, piercing eyes, and sleek and full appearance. However, no rush to think about a nuptial partner yet. A fellow has to play the field somewhat before committing. I never really noticed these fair morsels until recently, but that's all part of maturing.

Amazing how the daylight hours have lengthened, allowing more time for feeding as I continue to build strength. Over fifteen hours each day chasing food is certainly sufficient. Our particular salmon school is now abeam of Cape Spear heading south to Cape Race.

Depending on tide conditions, we traverse our way along the shore encountering currents caused by recent winds that slow our progress on occasion. Around certain areas we have free access to feed along shore with the absence of nets. This is a big break for us. Some fishers do not subscribe to gillnets as a means of harvesting cod. They rely on the more conservation-oriented methods of longlining and hand-lines, but that requires bait for the hooks used. They have to either buy the bait or catch it themselves and that requires more work and more initial cost. However, many other fishermen want to use gillnets to reduce cost and labour. In any event, the nets are my biggest problem.

We tend to remain closer to one another now in a more intimate and dedicated fashion, as if genetically inspired toward some common connubial denominator. Our paths are more definite, our intentions more clear. We have to reach this seemingly promised-land by a predetermined time.

The summer days are enjoyable as we proceed through the pelagic waters chasing food fish and gorging ourselves every opportunity we get. Some of the capelin have already come to land to propagate their species. Generously, nature has afforded copious prey on our last few weeks at sea. Yes, that's right, my marine home for the past twenty-six months will soon be vacated in favour of a freshwater environment again.

I have enjoyed the open expanse of the free-swimming marine environment. The world has been my oyster, so to speak. My migration has taken me off Greenland and down the Labrador coast. Flirting with warm and cold currents, thermoclines, icebergs, and the many predators have endowed me with great resiliency.

Why did I stay out here in the open ocean for over two years? Why am I now plodding my way back to a place yet unknown? What keeps me going? Of course it is not only me, but the rest of my school friends as well.

Do the females have that homing instinct and we males just follow? You fellows know what I mean, when a lady gets dressed up and the scent of her perfume permeates your olfactory lobes. Don't you want to follow her? Egotistically I would like to think I know my own way, but hey, I am not averse to being a follower.

Hard as nails we are. Splendid examples of nature's best. No room here for the weak of heart either. A sound mind and a sound body. Look at my dorsal muscles as they protrude exponentially from my tail to my anterior pectorals. Peer at the strength in my tail just posterior to the adipose fin, that vestigial organ common to Atlantic salmon.

It is no wonder that we have so many predators. Predators have captured many of my school that for one reason or another became unhealthy and did not have the ability to escape their clutches. Therefore, only the fittest of us remain. "Survival of the fittest," stated Darwin in his theory of evolution. Nature wants only the strongest of the species to produce young. Genetic strength is a prerequisite to future continuing generations. While we have a few among us showing net marks and scars, generally speaking our condition is superb. However, our pilgrimage is not ended and more exploits await us.

Placentia Bay, the largest bay in Newfoundland, is a fine hike. We arrive along the shoreline of the Burin Peninsula and then *La Voila*, St. Pierre et Miquelon. Have to be very careful around those French Islands because fishers there continue to be permitted to use gillnets to catch salmon. Situated as they are at the mouth of Fortune Bay, they are in a good geographical position to intercept us salmon as we migrate to our home rivers, none of which are on the French Islands. Perhaps before too long this commercial fishery can be halted to further protect us. However, soon we say *au revoir* and then *bienvenue* to Fortune Bay as Brunette Island and then Sagona Island heave into view.

These islands, once inhabited by fishermen and their families until the late fifties are now without human life. Brunette Island does have caribou and ptarmigan that appear to do well due to the lack of predators. Only the carrying capacity of the island limits their numbers. Bison were brought there in 1964, but this experiment did not turn out too well as these creatures require expanses of grassy plains, rather than the rocky and sheer cliffs on the island. It is surmised that most of them fell off the cliffs and into the sea. The island is still a sanctuary for animal studies by wildlife biologists.

As we enter Fortune Bay, a number of my comrades continue to travel north and west, presumably preconditioned for other destinations. Also, unlike me and my closest companions, a few others keep to the south of the bay while we take a more northerly route. They are probably destined for Grand Bank and Garnish Rivers.

The trip through Fortune Bay is not without mishap and we lose a few more companions. Every now and then we sight those cartilaginous wonders of the deep, sharks. No escaping those teeth. I encounter small schools of herring, a few lumpfish (easy to understand how they got their name because they look like a lump in the water), schools of capelin, and scattered cod that rise from the bottom to feed on capelin. We are a much diversified bunch out here in Fortune Bay, and I haven't mentioned all of them.

Schools of herring come directly into view every now and then as they appear to move in a wave-like pattern. They are probably waiting and seeking out coves in Fortune Bay in which to spawn later. Some herring spawn in the spring and others in the fall

I forgot to mention another amazing change that has taken place in my physical structure. It is not something that I am particularly proud of because it gives me a more fearful look. I refer to the protrusion of my lower jaw that now has an upward extension at the tip, somewhat like the downward extension on the upper beak of a bald eagle. I'm not sure why I've developed this protruding lower lip except to signify the complete acknowledgement of reaching the final stage of adulthood. I am now capable of reproducing. Females are sometimes associated with too much lip, but not so with us salmon. It is the males that have the most lip.

Adult salmon. (Atlantic Salmon Federation)

CHAPTER FIVE

DESTINATION RIVER AT LAST

Long Harbour River is isolated on the north side of Fortune Bay and only accessible by boat or air unless you want to undertake the journey by an all-terrain vehicle, and that is difficult. I have an affinity for that river, and along with my other comrades we head directly toward it. It is amazing how we have this innate ability to leave the open ocean and set sail for the river of birth. You humans certainly don't have that kind of attribute and getting lost appears to be a daily occurrence for many of you.

The entrance to Long Harbour River becomes a fjord about ten miles long, and as I travel through the channel the rougher marine setting gradually gives way to calmer waters. The many different species that had been found in the ocean become less diverse as we navigate and zigzag our way along the shoreline. We still see a number of herring and also encounter a few trout. We know that a number of speckled trout and brown trout do spend time in marine waters and return to the home river to spawn, but they do not journey far out into the ocean like we do.

Nestled among high hills, the gravity-fed river gradually meets the depths of the bay, forming a small tidal bore. Here in this place devoid of human habitation, I cogitate my next move as the silence is broken only infrequently by the sound of a fisherman's outboard motor. During the salmon angling season there is frequent boating activity as recreational fishermen converge on Long Harbour River hoping for success. On this day the local activity is relatively moderate, and the fjord is serenely calm except for the movement produced by the wake of an occasional passing boat.

I amble around the river's mouth as my body adapts to the less saline environment of the brackish water. This adjustment does not take too long, and very soon I will be ready to ascend my actual and aspired river-migration part of the journey. I will join a few of my companions as we begin our ascent. Right now it is time for a rest before starting our freshwater trip.

This ability to change from salt water to fresh water provides me the opportunity to take advantage of a more secure spawning habitat when compared to the marine setting. On the other hand, the ability to change from fresh water to marine in my younger years permitted me to enter an environment where growth is far better. Therefore, I have a double benefit compared to pure freshwater or pure saltwater fishes.

I can't explain how I do it, whether it is natural instinct or a combined biological compass, radar, sonar, and navigator, but anyway I am back in the river of my birth. Here again, in the influence of brackish water that I left a little over two years ago, I wait for a few days to acclimatize myself before starting the second leg of my anadromous migration. The volume of fresh water moving into the estuary indicates that there is a sufficient water level in the river for my ascent. However, I intend to wait for rain, even though some of my cohorts have already headed upstream. The higher the water levels in the river, the easier my upward migration will be.

As you probably know, after a rain it takes a day or two for the water level in the river to rise significantly, supplemented by the tributaries in the river watershed that feed into the main river. The amount of rain and the time period it falls have a dual effect on how long it takes the river to rise and how far it rises. However, I will take this into consideration as I contemplate my journey up Long Harbour River.

Long Harbour River has always been a good salmon-producing river. It has all the amenities necessary for success for it is a veritable maternity ward and pediatric centre. Anglers have long treasured this fishing spot and many return year after year to partake of this angling challenge and luxuriate in its precious solitude. Although the peacefulness of the river is sometimes broken by the sounds of helicopters and all-terrain vehicles, such interference is usually short-lived. However, those all-terrain people-movers have helped to increase angling pressure, and subsequently angling catches have decreased salmon populations.

The decline in salmon populations has led to further restrictions on recreational salmon fishing. Very restrictive regulations apply to bag limits, and 'catch and release' is applied in many areas. Of course, it is unlawful to retain parr and smolt, the so-called juvenile forms of our species.

The salmon pools in Long Harbour River have been favourite angling sites for many years. Mitchell's Pool, Seven Mile Pool and Twelve Mile Pool are well known to many enthusiastic sportsmen that frequent this site. Some of the anglers even set up camps during the summer on the river's edge to provide sleeping accommodation for use at their leisure. A few permanent structures for summer use have also been erected. Therefore, even though Long Harbour River is not accessible by road, there is much activity surrounding us when we begin the river migration and are navigating our way upstream during the summer.

Salmon angling is considered one of the greatest pleasures of life remaining today. Now that many people have more leisure time, the pressure on salmon streams is often overwhelming. Every angler appreciates the opportunity to cast an artificial fly on the fast-running water and anticipate a rise from one of us salmon. The angler casts the fly to the sounds of birds and the rushing of the water. He or she watches intently, waiting and then casting again, each time trying to land the fly in a particular spot in the river. She/he may tie on another fly when the first one appears to have exhausted its usefulness or has failed to entice a rise. After trying several flies without success, the angler still anticipates anxiously the moment when he or she can cry, "I've hooked one!"

Whoops, got carried away there for the moment. Almost wished I were an angler.

CHAPTER SIX

BEGINNING MY RIVER ASCENT

I didn't have to wait long for rain. On July 17 the downpour begins very early in the morning. On the rising tide, accompanied by about twenty or more companions, we start upriver but take time to rest in Mitchell's Pool, not far from the river mouth. Ten or twelve hours elapse before the river shows any appreciable difference in water levels from the falling rain. However, June has been treated with frequent rain showers so the water levels remain very suitable for our purpose.

The rain also brings out the anglers. They understand that rain usually stirs us to move upstream. All kinds of slickly-tied, artificial flies appear on the surface of our pool, encouraging a rise from us. There are dark flies, light ones, blue ones, red ones, and multi-colored specimens, some of which defy description. Jock Scott, Silver Doctor, Blue Charm, you name it, I've seen it. Since we rarely eat on our river ascent, my interest in flies is cursory. Those of us who express more than a casual interest often end up as victims.

The various artificial flies scooting over the water do torment us, and some salmon unwarily rise to the occasion after losing patience. Patience is really the answer to this duel, and the one who gives in first ends up the loser. The sportsman is matching his or her patience and wits with ours. My patience sometimes wears thin, but I continue to resist. I see more flies cast over me, but I wasn't born yesterday.

We often have to deal with the cunning angler as well. I speak of those who use the correct paraphernalia, but with dubious means. I include a person who because they can discern us in the pool, often try to manoeuvre the hook into our mouth. While this is not an easy task, it can happen, as a few of us have found out. It takes a combination of skill and luck for the angler.

Although such foul hooking is illegal, it is only small stuff compared to the use of jiggers. Those large hooks can rip into our sides and stomachs, causing lethal damage, and are the real scourge of us all. People who use those can be classified as recreational misfits, in that they don't deserve to be called anglers and also because they have no regard for conservation. I have heard stories of salmon that received scars from jiggers and succumbed to the injuries later. Fortunately I have not personally seen such method applied, but I'll cross my fins for good luck!

Throughout the day more and more salmon enter our pool as the tide rises and then begins to recede again, followed by another group on the second high tide. Since Mitchell's Pool is so close to the mouth of the river, a lot of salmon congregate here on the first lap of the upstream sojourn. There is a large number of anglers here too, with artificial flies everywhere on the surface of our resting pool, especially as the last few hours of daylight draw near. Dusk can't come quickly enough for me, as it takes all my time to maintain a safe position in the pool, apart from outdistancing those artificial flying insects. As darkness overtakes us, we slumber in our thoughts and await the next move.

The water temperature is about 15 degrees Centigrade, but the rain has a cooling effect. The combination of falling rain and flowing river helps to oxygenate the water. I find out that a fellow must be in good physical condition to withstand this segment of the migration. The distance we have to travel plus encounters with rapids, anglers, and falls are all energy-consuming activities. Sometimes we can get behind rocks in the river where the current is not as strong in order to save a little energy. Bet you didn't think those large rocks in the river are such an advantage for us, but they sure can be a physical shelter from fast-moving water, apart from dissipating the flow and temporarily lessening the speed of the current. We know how to use the course of the river to our benefit.

Next morning just at daybreak, the sound and sight of artificial flies landing on the surface of our pool can be heard again. There are a number of cabins adjacent to the pool and that provides ready and early access for anglers. However, I am determined to move farther upstream, and within an hour of first light, I am already on my way in concert with many of my compatriots.

We wind our way along following the contours of the river, stopping only briefly, and eventually we reach Seven Mile Pool. This is a fairly large area for convalescing after the trip from Mitchell's Pool and there is more room here to spread out. The water here is fairly fast and full of oxygen. You could say it is a breath of fresh air and a definite relief.

Once again though the anglers are busy, as we scatter behind the rocks along the length of the pool in an effort to shelter ourselves. The cascading water has over the years managed to provide enough force to disturb the bottom and provide shelter for us in relatively deep water. It appears that the anglers here are experienced and know exactly where to cast their flies, even though the ice and strong currents of the past early spring engineered changes in the river and gave us different places to rest. We move around in the pool just to make it a little more difficult for them.

There are a few anglers that have no angling attributes at all. I mention one fellow who is sitting on a rock overhanging our small pool with his shoes and socks off, dangling his feet in the water and casting his line immediately over us. I could have bitten his toes, he was so close. If all anglers were like him, we would have no worries, but at least his feet were clean.

Then again, many recreational anglers are just content to have the opportunity to partake in salmon fishing purely as a recreational activity. Often with a few buddies, or even spouses, they spend some time fishing from the bank of the river on a sunny day supplemented with a cooked meal outdoors and a few shots of rum or whiskey. It is a great experience if so inclined, but you need indelible patience for the actual fishing part. Don't mistake me, there are really good female anglers too who also may imbibe as well.

This pool is a favourite spot for salmon because of its size, the rate of water flow, and the diversity of the sheltering places. Even so, we still have to be careful of those artificial-flying-abnormalities landing close every now and again. They try to make those artificial flies closely resemble real insects, but we have to smile to ourselves when we see some of them. There is no insect that ever looked like some of those artificial beasts. Imaginations gone wild.

Fly-fishing may go back to the second century, but in the 1600s there appears to have been fishing activities recorded in Britain. It has also been reported in Japan, North America, Norway, and Australia. The practice of fly-tying is conducted by individuals, but can also be a commercial operation. Various items are used to tie flies, such as feathers from a variety of birds, hair from different animals, as well as synthetic materials. Fly-tying also requires much patience, observation, and ingenuity.

The type of fly-fishing here on Long Harbour River and many other areas is called dry-fly fishing. The nomenclature refers to the fact that the line and fly float on the water and the angler has to be adept to keep it moving that way. The rod used is light and flexible with a reel to hold the yards of fishing line, and it takes the skill of the angler to master the art of casting and retrieval.

You can see from the effort applied that I have to be very agile and intelligent to outwit all those recreational fishermen who spend much time and effort to catch me. Consequently, here I am still going strong with no intention of losing the battle.

CHAPTER SEVEN

FIRST REAL MISHAP

It was one of those days when I am behaving myself just riding along in the current with a number of other salmon, but it is a more shallow part of the pool. Anglers have been busy since daylight casting flies above our heads. It looks like another routine day when suddenly I feel a sting on my tail and very soon I find myself being pulled backward and this is not the usual way for me to swim. An angler has somehow managed to hook an artificial fly in my tail section just ahead of my caudal fin and my movement in trying to escape has only succeeded in wrapping the monofilament line around my tail. This type of hooking happens infrequently, but I am now a victim of such an occurrence. It is of course an illegal way to hook us salmon.

I try with all my might to pull away, but the hook only appears to become more embedded and the line around me is cutting into the flesh of my tail section. Even though my tail is hooked, I still manage to make a few leaps out of the water trying to engineer a release. However, all this activity on my part is only making matters worse, but I have no intention of giving up easily.

Then I decide to go deep in the pool behind a rock and stay there. I figure by going deep the angler will try to lift me and possibly haul out the hook or break the line. Not so, this guy knows how to handle every move that I make, and I begin to feel negative about my predicament.

The initial ordeal lasts about half an hour, and my effort is still not looking favourable. The angler is maintaining a steady pressure on the line and the leaps I continue to make out of the water do nothing to facilitate an escape. I am becoming exhausted, and the hook is still embedded with about a foot of the line wrapped around my tail. The taut line also hampers my tail movement, and along with sapping my energy, it is now very difficult for me to move at all.

Try as I might, I am unable to stop my movement toward shore as the angler begins reeling me in, foot by foot, in a very cautious way. The angler does not even know I am hooked by the tail until I come much closer to him. Finally as I near the shore he gets the dip-net ready for the concluding part of the capture. My dreams are coming to an end as I feel myself lifted in the net. The hook is removed from my tail with care and the line untangled. Then much to my surprise I am placed back in the river, my sides gently rubbed before finally being released. I'm not sure whether the angler is an honest fisherman or if the sudden appearance of a fisheries enforcement official biased the outcome. Nevertheless, I am grateful and will never forget this journey through Seven Mile Pool. The scars on my tail remain as a reminder but they will heal.

CHAPTER EIGHT

UPSTREAM JOURNEY CONTINUES

Many people are becoming concerned about the decline in our populations. New regulations require anglers to release large salmon because the larger we are, the more eggs are produced, and therefore more salmon progeny to facilitate our chances for success. Organizations are promoting our well-being by advocating what can be done to conserve our species. All are dedicated to the conservation, protection, and restoration of Atlantic salmon, including our habitat or the ecosystems in which we live, be it marine or freshwater.

Time to move on again. The weather is warmer, and I require a sufficient volume of water for comfortable ascent. I encounter a falls, but it's not high enough to cause a real problem, so along with my companions we leap over it effortlessly. However, just about a mile beyond is another more than twice as high that causes us to stop.

I have to assess this situation. It's just as well to rest until nightfall and continue my travels early next morning. As dusk disappears into night, I contemplate the jump over the falls as a new day finally rolls around. Mustering all my energies, I move downstream from the falls. Then with shark speed I head for the falls and at the final instant unleash my strong tail, becoming airborne. Dejected, I fall back in failure, but some of my companions are successful on the first try and a few more on the second attempt.

For my second attempt I select a jump site with less turbulence at the bottom of the falls. This time I leave no stone unturned as I speed toward the falls and make the leap. As I struggle to the top of the falls in full flight, I feel like an athlete breaking an Olympic record. Landing with a splash at the top of the falls, my rapid body movements propel me into smoother water and away from the precipice of the falls. The obstacle has been conquered and I pound my chest with my pectoral fins.

I don't know why we go through so much adversity to climb and jump over falls. Why don't we just spawn below the falls instead of navigating upstream for many miles? Why are some fish satisfied to spawn in the lower reaches of the river while others like me prefer the upper reaches? What drives some of us to greater heights? While watching us jump over falls may be entertaining for onlookers, it is a chore for us salmon. We do put on a good show as we leap over falls, literally flying through the air, up, up and away. However, jumping falls is not a good practice when bears are around. Those beasts just stand at the top of the falls and nab us when we land in a vulnerable position, but there are no bears today so we can relax.

Upward I swim until I reach Twelve Mile Pool. Anglers are busy here too, in this veritable fishing haven completely isolated from the everyday worries of the world. Tents have been put up and helicopters used to ferry people in and out of the area. Here, twelve miles up from the river mouth, a recreational fishing community has been created for the sole purpose of salmon angling. This is a good compromise to get away from it all and match wits with us salmon. Only your closest friends will know where you are.

Yarns are told by anglers about the abundance of salmon on Long Harbour River in the sixties and seventies. A large number of photos are available to substantiate what often appears at first to be exaggeration. There are photographs giving documented proof of up to seven salmon jumping falls at the same time. Yarns are told about hooking and releasing over twenty fish in less than two hours. Those were the days of more fish and fewer anglers, and when most fishermen exhibited a greater degree of honesty. Nowadays you hear more stories of anglers openly breaking fishing laws in their quest to obtain salmon. I suppose it is the competition associated with the large numbers of people taking up salmon fishing coupled with fewer salmon. They often engage in the sport without being indoctrinated concerning conservation. It becomes something to do in their spare time for the short term. No real regard for the future of salmon, or in many cases, the environment.

People will have to learn to live with nature in a mutually considerate fashion rather than continue to show dominance at the expense of other creatures. Long Harbour River is a good place to start because it is untouched by industry, and only the human frailties require correction and guidance.

One specimen that can aggravate our ascent on occasion is that busy, four-legged creature with the sharp incisor teeth and flat tail known as the beaver. Dams are built on rivers by them that are prime examples of animal engineering. They cut down large trees and position them across narrow places in the river before filling in the holes with branches, rocks, and mud that often leads to major flooding of the area. Those dams make it difficult if not impossible for us to navigate upstream. Sometimes, when sufficient water is flowing over the dam, we can jump the structure. Other times wildlife officers have to break open the dams to allow us passage, but in most cases the beavers can have the dam repaired within hours. However, even this intermittent reprieve can give us a window of opportunity to continue our movement upstream.

Dams built on rivers and streams are not only beneficial to beavers, but can also provide excellent feeding places and shelter for trout species. The dams help to trap food items floating downstream and often flood adjoining areas to offer new habitat. As parr we often used those deeper pools of water resulting from beaver dams for food supplies and for overwintering as a form of safe refuge. You could say we have learned to live in symbiotic relationship with beavers. Yes they may block our upward migration on occasion, but very seldom with dire consequences.

Incidentally, many salmon do not go to sea because for some reason or other, usually the result of human activity, they have become landlocked and deprived of access to the sea. Those salmon are called 'landlocked salmon or ouananiche' and are found in many lakes in Canada and other North Atlantic regions.

As I start to overtake the upper reaches of the river, the water becomes less rapid in movement. Tributary streams are more frequent as they bifurcate from the basin area. Long Harbour River is more placid at this juncture, and the gravity flow is somewhat less because of the reduced river gradient.

The adult stage of Atlantic salmon after returning to the river from the sea. (Atlantic Salmon Federation)

CHAPTER NINE

MY BIRTHPLACE AGAIN

The next day I proceed upriver for only a short distance before stopping, as if I am aware my destination has finally been reached. During my ascent over the past number of days, sections of the river are familiar to me, but none as recognizable as my present location. The expansive gravel area appears to be suitable for my near-future plan. A steady flow of running water fifty centimetres deep (about eighteen inches) is the norm. Without ceremony, I know I am home at last in the place of my birth. It so happens that this particular part of the river is home for approximately fifteen others as well.

The wonders of salmon migration that take us back to our home rivers are as yet unexplained in many respects. I left the Atlantic Ocean and have the navigational instincts to return to the exact place where I was hatched. What a feat! I'm glad my companions share my attributes in that regard as well.

Sure, you humans can approximate this same feat with various navigational instruments, but I inherently have all these capabilities. You who are supposed to be the intelligent ones, the so-called higher forms of life. Many still possess some of this innate ability because you like to return to your birthplace at least once during your lifetime. Then some of you never leave it. Anyway, enough bragging for now.

As I completed my marine sojourn and ascended the river, I underwent certain physical changes. My silver sheen has grown progressively less noticeable, and the deep blue shine on my dorsal area has turned somewhat darker. My bottom jaw has developed the hook complemented with larger and sharper teeth. My whole exterior appearance that offered pride and protection has metamorphosed into a condition conducive to propagation. My somewhat mottled look blends in with the variously coloured gravel in the riverbed and I am not as discernible to the naked eye. My colour also helps me blend in with the seemingly darker water as the sun's rays beam from a lower position in the sky and offer more protection for what lies ahead.

For the present I will savour the solitude of this quiet river, free of molestation, just as my ancestors enjoyed and utilized it for centuries. As the nights gradually become cooler and the late summer fades into autumn, certain avian friends find themselves heading south. The warm days and nights change to less warm days and cooler nights. More frequent rain showers in early morning quickly turn to fine weather as daylight signals the start of each day.

The clear blue skies, so familiar to the area during the fall, provide a perfect background to my river home. Hunters replace anglers as the annual search for the elusive moose begins in earnest. It is a time when salmon get a well-deserved rest and let our four-legged friends take the recreational heat. Not much rest for wildlife in general though, as more and more people have more and more time to hunt and fish.

Autumn is a beautiful time of year with its myriad of colours as deciduous trees fall prey to oncoming winter conditions. The conifers retain their summer greenness, except for the tamarack, to provide background for the spectrum of other colours, just as you would arrange plants in a vase. The sun's rays cascade over our potential breeding ground, completely masking our identity in the rippling beams of light and the movement of the water.

The more frequent fall showers help to enrich our oxygen supply. The anglers have long gone, along with their continual 'flogging' of Long Harbour River, but we are sometimes startled by the occasional all-terrain vehicles that carry hunters.

The odd black bear poses a threat whenever they happen upon us during a crossing and they don't use a rod and artificial fly either. No sir, just one bob of their head and dinner is ready. We manage to stay in relatively deep water where we are more difficult to be seen by the bears. Moose often enter the edges of our river, but luckily they eat vegetation and are true vegans.

All is in readiness for a major event, an event that has social consequences and even economic considerations for a large number of people. It is also an event that has significant repercussions for the future of Atlantic salmon. The 'King of Fishes' has reached maturity! Nothing can stand in my way now. The urge to propagate is about to reach its climax. Two years at sea have provided me the greatest gift of all, and that is the opportunity to give life to new salmon offspring.

Fully mature, I celebrate my gonadal accomplishment and stake out my territory as do other of my male friends. We swim back and forth as if in a stupor, finally taking charge and splitting off in different directions. My conjugal fate is reaching a conclusion.

I have been swimming around with a female companion who graciously reacts to my enthusiasm. Her amorous approaches kindle a flame, and I unfailingly stick by her side. Then, suddenly during late afternoon, she stretches on her side and with beatings of her tail above the river-bed causes the gravel to dislodge and form a small depression. After a few more strokes of her tail it becomes a redd. How did she know what to do?

With both of us steadied over the redd, she lays about two-hundred eggs and I hurriedly and proudly fertilize them. She then covers the eggs with gravel, again by using her tail, and it forms a small mound on the riverbed. We go through this process twice more so I'm thinking at least six-hundred eggs must now be located on the river-bed. Our efforts now over, impregnation awaits. Other mating salmon in our river area also perform this ritual until thousands of eggs are deposited and fertilized and a number of redds can be seen. In my case, her genes and mine are left to contribute to a new generation of offspring. The cycle of life has been completed. It is a fitting culmination to a very meagre and austere beginning that with thoughtfulness will have no end.

My female partner and I have been drained of all life-giving substances. In our cycle of life we have endured our early years in Long Harbour River, travelled downstream to the sea, braved the north Atlantic, escaped predators, manoeuvred around nets, outwitted anglers, and leaped over falls to fulfill our final obligations. The Atlantic salmon species has been given another chance for survival. We can do nothing more.

Much now depends on environmental conditions as the fertilized eggs lay dormant. Tiny eggs covered with gravel to protect them from external life-threatening conditions will be held *in situ* until next spring. Transferring the genetic material that will give the characteristics to our offspring is the first stage of development. Imagine all that taking place without any help from anyone. Life is being created from each single egg that is impregnated by my sperm cells. Development will be slow, but as long as conditions on the riverbed remain satisfactory, the end will justify the means. The eggs in the redd will have to contend with ice and large pieces of wood among other things that often disrupt the river bottom, but Long Harbour River has been the birthplace of salmon for many, many years, and I anticipate my progeny to be successful.

You probably have not heard an Atlantic salmon tell his own life story before, but I Salmo, thought it was time to relate it. The same story can be told on many different rivers year after year. As long as we can continue our spawning ritual, our species will be kept off the endangered list. But we are being stretched to the limit mainly through human influence. We conquer many obstacles to do our share, but your support is of utmost importance.

Incidentally, many Atlantic salmon live to spawn again. Now that you know more about me, Salmo, I will leave the final outcome of my particular fate to your own imagination.

CLASSIFICATION OR TAXONOMY OF ATLANTIC SALMON

Phylum:	Chordata
Class:	Osteichthyes
Order:	Salmoniformes
Family:	Salmonidae
Genus:	Salmo
Species:	salar

Chordata refers to animals with a backbone or spinal cord. Osteichthyes are bony fishes as opposed to those that have cartilage, like sharks. Salmoniformes means bony fishes like salmon, trout, whitefishes, and others found in both freshwater and marine waters. Salmonidae is a type of salmoniformes that have soft fins and includes fishes such as salmon and trout. Salmo and salar classifies Atlantic salmon directly as the genus and species and is the nomenclature you will most often see used for them when referenced: *Salmo salar*. Another genus and species is *Salmo trutta*, or brown trout.

Terms Used

Fins. The most forward bottom fins are the pectorals; the middle bottom fins are the ventrals; the bottom fin near the tail is the anal; the big fin on the back is the dorsal; the small protrusion on the back near the tail is the adipose fin (although not really a fin); and the tail fin is the caudal.

Grilse. Salmon that have been at sea for at least one winter and may weigh up to one and one half kilos.

Book Three

THE WHALES AT POINT AU GAUL

Gordon Snow

This book is dedicated to those who assisted in the attempt to release as many pilot whales as possible from the beach at Point au Gaul in July 1979. It showed the willingness to participate against great odds and also demonstrated the frailty of human effort that sometimes accompanies environmental tragedy.

ACKNOWLEDGEMENTS

Special thanks to Bill and Clara Tibbo and Lou Ryan for a number of the images used and Fisheries and Oceans Canada for some of the statistics.

INTRODUCTION

There are many unexplained happenings in nature, and that is what makes biology so interesting. The plight of a pod of pilot whales as told in this story is but one of them. It emphasizes the fact that more study and explanation is required concerning the many creatures that inhabit the earth, especially those in the marine environment. The oceans are home to the largest vertebrate, (animal with a backbone) the blue whale, and the largest invertebrate (animal without a backbone), the giant squid. The world's oceans and seas are ecosystems within ecosystems and much is still unknown.

It is also interesting that the blue whale is a baleen whale, feeding mainly on euphausiids (shrimp-like creatures) that are filtered from the water by the coarse bristles of the baleen in their upper jaws. The blue whale grows to over twenty-seven metres long and can weigh over 150 tons. At birth, blue whales are seven to eight metres long and weigh two to three tons. In about seven months, the rich milk supplied by the mother allows them to grow to a length of sixteen metres and weigh twenty-five tons. They have been protected since 1966.

Whales were hunted on the east coast of Canada in the late 1500s by the Basques in the Strait of Belle Isle area. During the following seventeenth through to the nineteenth century whaling was conducted by the French, British, and Americans, as well as by Canadians; aboriginal people were also involved, but mainly for subsistence. The Norwegians began whaling in Newfoundland in 1898, and in 1902 the Newfoundland government established the Whaling Industry Act for conservation reasons. The industry continued until 1972 in both

Newfoundland and Labrador and Nova Scotia. During the period 1946 to 1972, almost 64,000 whales were landed in the two provinces with 96 percent occurring in Newfoundland and Labrador. Pilot whales made up the bulk of the total landings (85 percent), followed by fin whales (11 percent); other whales taken included blue, humpback, sei, sperm, minke, and killer. The last blue whale taken in Newfoundland and Labrador was in 1951.

The International Whaling Commission (IWC) was established under the International Convention for the Regulation of Whaling and was signed in 1946. The IWC voted to put a moratorium on whaling in 1982 with enforcement scheduled for 1986. Canada left the IWC in 1982, but whaling is banned except for aboriginal people in northern regions.

Presently, the major activity relating to whales is whale watching. This has become a major pastime and tourist attraction in many areas of the world, especially as ecotourism expands. There appears to be worldwide acceptance for the need to conserve whales, but strandings by pilot whales may be something that will remain out of our control and will continue to be a natural phenomenon.

As Area Manager, my interest and involvement in this story related to the responsibility for marine mammals under the Canadian Department of Fisheries and Oceans *Fisheries Act.*

Author

CHAPTER ONE

THE INITIAL BEACHING

It was Saturday, July 14, 1979, and I was up at five thirty a.m. anticipating a planned helicopter patrol to observe the water levels of rivers on the Burin Peninsula, located on the south coast of Newfoundland in the province of Newfoundland and Labrador on Canada's east coast. The annual upstream migration of Atlantic salmon was now taking place on all rivers, and determining sufficient water levels to permit this anadromous species to succeed in their migration was important. Exceptionally low water levels could lead to closure of recreational fishing. When water levels are low, the salmon are often held up in pools along the rivers and are more vulnerable to potential poaching or natural death. However, closing a salmon river to angling is a last resort.

At around six twenty a.m. my phone rang, and as I placed the receiver to my ear I expected to hear one of the Fishery officers on the line. Instead it was the excited voice of Albert Dodge exclaiming that a large number of whales were ashore at Point au Gaul. His knowledge of whale sightings and his description were all that was necessary to determine that they were pilot whales, commonly called 'potheads.' Albert reckoned there were between 130 and 150 altogether. All thoughts of flying vanished as Albert gave as much detail as possible from his cursory observation that morning.

Point au Gaul is a small community on the southern part of the Burin Peninsula. It is about twenty-six kilometres from Grand Bank where I am located as Area Manager for the Canadian Department of Fisheries and Oceans. Point au Gaul like most communities on the Burin Peninsula, is a fishing community with around one hundred residents. On this day, the whales outnumbered the residents.

Fisheries and Oceans Canada has jurisdiction over living marine mammals as well as fish and shellfish, including the environment and habitat in which they live. Whales, seals, and walruses are thus covered under the Canadian *Fisheries Act* and its accompanying regulations.

Pilot whales (*Globicephala melaena*) are relatively abundant around Newfoundland and Labrador as well as along all of the Atlantic coast of Canada. They are referred to as one of the toothed whale species collectively called odontocetes. The others are the baleen whales that lack teeth and are in a group called mysticetes. Male pilot whales can be considerably larger than females with lengths over six metres and weighing up to three tons. These whales usually travel in large pods and are frequently found where squid are congregated. Females are mature at about six years while males take about twelve years. The gestation period is between fifteen and sixteen months. Birthing occurs in the period May to November, and calves may take up to two years to be weaned.

Groundings or beachings are not uncommon for pilot whales, but over one hundred was sure a large pod. I assured Albert we would be on the scene as soon as possible.

A phone call to Fishery Officer Berkley Slade soon led to changing our previous plans and had us motoring to Point au Gaul, arriving at about seven fifteen a.m. Many of the residents of the community had been alerted to the presence of their unusual visitors and with much dismay stood on the shoreline staring at the large black mammals as they thrashed about on the beach.

Early morning scene.
(G. Snow)

What a colossal confusion existed as we observed the large mammals, many of them completely high and dry on the beach, stranded but fighting for their lives. Others were still partly afloat with their tails splashing vertically in and out of the water, a subdued groaning echoing out from a number of them in a last-ditch effort for survival. In an attempt to work their way to open water, they hurled their bodies against rocks, bringing blood to injured appendages. Tails of some hit tails of others causing subsequent damage. The water turned red with blood as the waves washed up on the beach in the continuous ebb and flow. A couple of female whales could be seen bleeding profusely, indicating a probable cessation of what would have been an otherwise usual, natural birthing occurrence. It appeared that the females tried to deliver their young knowing they would probably die themselves. In any event, a number of fetuses were visible along the shoreline, but they were all fatalities and from all appearances, definitely premature.

A few of the larger whales beached on the rocks.
(G. Snow)

It shows the determination that a mother animal displays when something unusual happens and interferes with the natural birthing procedure. Premature births occur in many animal species and for different reasons. There are many cases where a baby is delivered while the mother ends up as a fatality. It could have been in this case that the traumatic effect of the beaching caused the premature births, or perhaps it was a last-ditch effort by the pregnant female pilot whales to deliver their babies, knowing they would succumb to an untimely death. In this case, neither the mothers nor the babies survived the ordeal.

A rocky ending.
(G. Snow)

Young whales that were born only to die.
(G. Snow)

Berkley and I stood on a large rock contemplating our next move as the greyish morning turned to a brighter daylight. Although Berkley was an experienced Fishery Conservation Officer and had been involved in many job-related situations, this would be a new encounter for both him and me. We studied the surroundings and discussed options that would lead to our next moves.

A strong swell pounded on the beach and shoved the whales against the rocks, only to subside, leaving more of them high and dry. It was obvious we had to prioritize the extent of the whale beaching and make a decision on which whales would have the best chance of becoming free and entering the open sea again. Surveying the scene led us to the conclusion that less than one-third of the animals would fit into that category. We determined what action to take for specific whales, based on the location of them on the beach, the size of each whale and their visible condition. Only the fittest would be given assistance under the circumstances, but it had nothing to do with Darwin's survival of the fittest theory.

How long had the whales been on the beach by now? We met Albert on the beach and according to him, he is usually awakened by his biological clock to get ready for fishing. It was about four thirty a.m. he told us when he vacated the comfort of his bed to begin a new day. After arising, he looked through his window to observe the conditions of the sky, to try and ascertain in his own mind the probable weather for the day. On this particular early morning, conditions were far from ideal, and he was in no rush so he slowly went about the task of preparing breakfast. No engines could be heard, which signified that no other fishermen had left the cove this morning either. After completing a few chores, he went outside to get a better feel for the weather and obtain a closer look at sea and wind conditions.

The sky did not look good and water conditions were no better so it appeared to be another lost fishing day, or at least part of it. All the fishermen in Point au Gaul had basically reached the same conclusion. Albert further related to Berkley and me, "I looked out to the sea but peculiar sounds emanating from the direction of the beach caught my attention. It was certainly not the usual morning sounds with which I was familiar. In the grey mist, I tried to discern the origins of the sounds while approaching the beach. Then the awesome sight finally came into view. Whales! Lots of them. The presence of the whales was overwhelming. I had encountered whales many times while conducting fishing operations and was familiar with the sight of them, but that was in the open sea. This was an entirely unexpected and unexplained occurrence. It was after that I decided to call you."

Albert, like many other fellow fishers in the area, had fished from the shores of Point au Gaul and nearby Lamaline for years, as their forefathers had for centuries. Knowledge of the fishing grounds, physical geography, and geomorphology of the shoreline and offshore islands had been passed down to them as apprentices from an early age. They know all about calm seas, stormy seas, tides, and currents. Loss of life at sea had been witnessed. Day after day they plied their fishing trade, harvesting the riches of the sea. In a way they competed with whales for a number of the fish species in the area. However, Albert like his colleagues, observed whales with awe as they often encountered them migrating through their fishing area. Until some occurrence like this happens, pilot whales were considered by Albert and other fishing crews as just another sighting and, although common, nevertheless always interesting. His thoughts and feelings revealed to us that there was heartfelt anguish and he would much rather be watching them in their natural surroundings than contemplating their fate on the beach.

On this morning Albert and his fishing colleagues were surrounded by pilot whales inshore on a beach rather than on the fishing grounds. They were out of their element and introduced a new dimension. What could Albert and his fishing companions do to help?

Oddly enough, all of the whales in the pod did not end up on the beach. We could see a small pod of whales swimming offshore, but could not determine the number. They were most likely the whales swimming at the tail end of the initial pod. They must have realized what was happening to their contemporaries and managed to avoid the beaching. However, their instinct was also telling them not to leave the area, at least not yet.

CHAPTER TWO
IMMEDIATE ACTION

It is obvious that Albert's fellow citizens in Point au Gaul shared similar feelings about this unscheduled phenomenon. Nothing like this had ever happened in such close proximity to them. It was perplexing to visualize the scene in front of them of the dying whales. It seemed so out of place. So here we were, all pondering the next move with time being of the essence. As the saying goes, time and tide wait for no man, and in this case the tides were indeed important in any rescue attempt.

A few of the whales that had come ashore on a sandy part of the beach were already showing no recognizable signs of life. The sand may have penetrated their blowholes and interfered with their breathing. These whales were on the inside part of the beach and were probably leading the pod when they first beached on the high tide. We decided to try and free those whales farthest out on the beach as a first form of action. Some of them were still in shallow water but appeared to display most movement. Those we determined to be the strongest, along with the smallest, would have first opportunity for survival because we knew we could not even attempt to save them all. A few of the whales were small enough to be lifted out to freedom by two people, but not many were in that category.

Aerial view.
(Lou Ryan)

Close-up of two specimens.
(Bill and Clara Tibbo)

The beached mammals ranged between three and six metres in length with weights up to one metric tonne, although most were between four to five metres. They are the long-finned pilot whales that are relatively abundant along the Atlantic coast of Canada. Pilot whales (sometimes called blackfish as well as potheads) can be very gregarious. When they encounter squid prey, you can observe them in a real frenzy as they leap from the water or churn around on the surface while gorging themselves. Sightings around the coast of Newfoundland during summer and early fall often result from their pursuit of squid.

These whales through some quirk of nature had found themselves separated from their natural marine habitat during their migration and strayed to an area foreign to them. Although they are mammals like humans, they are as much in danger out of the water as we are in it.

We notice three small whales beached in fairly shallow water, but unless action can be taken quickly, they will not last too much longer in this world. Soliciting ready help from fishermen and other residents, we waded into the water and headed for the smaller potheads. The small creatures were manhandled and guided out to sea. On the first couple of releases they headed back toward us as if drawn by some parental instinct located on shore. Indeed, their mothers may have been on the shore and fully grounded. Subsequently they did swim off, flopping their tails on the water as if to say, thank you and goodbye.

Having done all we could with releasing the smaller whales, our attention turned to larger specimens. We selected those nearest to open water and still showing fairly good signs of life. The handling of the larger whales proved more awesome and downright dangerous. The strength in their tails made handling difficult and was certainly too much for us to cope with when they became agitated. When they begin thrashing their tails, we can only stand back until they calmed down again. We wait until the incoming waves pound ashore to provide each whale more buoyancy before trying to steer them out to sea. Then on the following wave we give a heave-ho, exerting all our strength like trying to launch a boat. Unknowingly and ironically, each whale in trying to do its best to escape was inadvertently assuring its demise by competing against our efforts. If only it could understand, but unfortunately there are very few whale whisperers. Also, if whales portrayed tail mobility and propulsion like finfish, it would be easier to propel themselves to open water. The pounding of their tails in vertical motion in shallow water was of no help and served to inflict self-injury. Many of them became exhausted in the ordeal. A creature weighing almost a ton and buoyant in its regular marine environment was certainly not very much at home in shallow water. These mammals of the sea require an extensive marine habitat to satisfy their daily requirements and propagate their species. They are familiar with spending their time in far deeper water along the continental slopes and beyond.

We continue to traverse the beach and give assistance, selecting the ones showing the strongest signs of life, outwardly. After about two hours of vital attempts, we have exhausted our worth. In our own exuberance in helping the whales to safety, we are often caught in an incoming wave that comes over the tops of our thigh boots. Wet from head to toe, we have to think of other means to complement human help.

This whale has some fight left in it.
(Bill and Clara Tibbo)

CHAPTER THREE

FIGHTING AGAINST THE TIDE

There was thought given to the potential use of a helicopter as a means to lift the whales to open water. However, after weighing the list of requirements, the weather, and the logistics of such an operation, it was discounted. Another aspect was that the noise of a helicopter operating in the area could cause the remaining part of the pod in the bay to become agitated and lead to further beachings.

The tide today in Point au Gaul was high at 0140 hrs and low at about 0740 hrs NDT (Newfoundland Daylight Time).The pilot whales were surmised to have become trapped somewhere between 0200 and 0400 hrs on the falling tide. This was the worst possible scenario for many of the whales that first beached themselves because it meant they would be out of the water for more than six hours between the falling and rising tides. We were now operating in the rising tide phase, which would peak again at 1340 hrs. Any possibility of further survival would have to be started by that time. After that it would again be a downhill battle against the falling tide. We knew as well that the potential to save any more of the whales, even on the rising tide, would be an onerous task from observations of their positions and physical condition along the beach. Any of the whales not off the beach during the lowering tide would end their lives there.

After speaking with a few of the fishermen, it was decided to use a number of motorized boats as well as rowboats and a few seemed to have shown up voluntarily anyway. The rough seas earlier in the day had precluded assistance from boats, and even now the fishermen of Point au Gaul will experience difficulty because of the location of the whales and the shallow water depths leading from the shoreline. The sea is still relatively rough, but not like earlier in the day. However, fishers and boat owners from the nearby community of Lamaline collaborated to assist their fellow fishers from Point au Gaul in the recovery effort. Armed with ropes and eager men, the boats stood ready on the scene to assist in the continuing battle for whale survival.

**Boats engaged in pulling whales from the shore to open water.
(Bill and Clara Tibbo)**

Another concern that we had was the pod of potheads still present in the bay and in no immediate danger. Although there was no way of knowing what they were thinking, it was our opinion they were waiting for their comrades to join them before moving farther out to sea. Our hope was that they too, would not come near enough to shore and strand themselves. We also anticipated this pod would provide a lure for those we were releasing from the beach. Some of the whales already released appeared to join the pod, while others did not, at least not immediately. It was thought that many of the younger whales would seek out their mothers as a first instinct, but may see some enticement to join the pod if the former were not an option. Then again, we were dealing with animals that are very much disoriented at this point in time and out of their natural element. Fishers could not remember ever seeing whales in this inshore location before now.

It is amazing how fast news travels, but word of the stranded whales was bringing people to the site from all around the Burin Peninsula. Cars lined the roadway on both sides as occupants hurried to the beach to view the event and capture it on film. Movie cameras rolled and shutters released to perpetuate the antics surrounding what could become a great marine disaster. The sheer number of onlookers indicated it was not a usual beaching and was probably one of the largest pods of beached pilot whales ever recorded in the North Atlantic.

Onlookers view the late afternoon scene.
(Bill and Clara Tibbo)

New Zealand has recorded many pilot whale mishaps like this, and there has been consideration given to the issue of strandings as being a predictor of earthquakes. Apparently, earthquakes have occurred very shortly after whales become stranded in various areas of the Pacific Ocean. Whales are thought to use a type of sonar (sound waves) to help them move around in the oceans. Therefore, early earth movements from a potential earthquake site may impede the sonar mechanisms of whales and cause them to mistakenly run upon beaches. It would also be plausible to assume that the occurrence of earthquakes can cause whale strandings. There is a difficulty however, in determining cause and effect. Whether whale strandings can predict earthquakes is open to question, as is the idea of earthquakes causing them. It is not as simple as the canary in the coal mine situation where the canary can give a warning to miners of impending exposure to methane gas and potential explosions.

Everything is in readiness to continue with our whale survival work. Each boat releases a rope toward the shore where it is tended by two men. These men select the fittest animals and secure the rope to the tail. We know that towing the whales by the tail could be detrimental to them so we select only those of smaller size that are located in adequate water depth. Upon signal, the boat's motor or the oarsmen will start gradually taking in slack until the whale itself begins moving seaward. The heavy beasts give sporadic thrusts with their tails as they move into deeper water. The operators of the boats release the ropes from the whales' tails after they become seaborne. This is a dangerous part of the ordeal because it has to be done by hand and done quickly. Nobody wants to be on the receiving end of one of those tail manoeuvres, and the whales are excited each time one of them gains the freedom of the open water again. On a few occasions the whales display too much enthusiasm and it prevents the operator in the boat from untying them. In those cases, the rope is severed with a knife, leaving a piece of it attached. Each time a whale is freed and swims away, there's spontaneous shouting from people onshore. Each whale released is considered by onlookers as an achievement.

One by one, each tow is completed as the tide becomes high and starts to ebb again. The motorboats struggle against the seas and the weight of their tow. Fishers and others engaged in the operation continue their selection and roping process. Even though many people congregate in our area, there's no interference, and everyone is content to take pictures and watch the proceedings. At about half low tide, the beached whales are rapidly being left without water. Finally, as a result of the total effort for the day, we had successfully towed or delivered forty potheads out to sea to give them opportunity for renewed life. Forty out of one hundred and thirty-nine is the extent of our whale survival operation.

We had worked the seas and tides to the best of everyone's ability and it was sad and very disheartening to watch many of the whales still on the beach and alive. It was a helpless feeling. A few of the younger people took it upon themselves to use buckets and pails to splash water over any whales now left on the beach but still showing signs of life, a sort of palliative care for those dying creatures. Young and old alike displayed grief for the dying and dead elephants of the sea that were now left abandoned on the shore. People passed by them as though paying last respects as if the whales were lying in state. Many onlookers can be seen reaching out in awe to touch the dying mammals.

It is amazing to watch and at the same time realize the strength of those mammoths when in their ocean environment compared to the helplessness they now endure. They have been part of the ocean ecosystem and travelled many miles during migration without difficulty, only to succumb to a fate like this. How long will such tragedies continue to occur?

A fisherman and I watched as one of the last whales swam to freedom in open water. We can see that a few of the released whales had formed a small pod separate from the main pod that continued to swim around just offshore. The whales in the new pod began moving toward a net owned by one of the fishermen. In a seemingly unpardonable action toward the fisherman who had helped refloat them, the mammals hit the net and put it out of fishing order. Most likely it would cause the fisherman some time and expense to repair the net. It didn't show much thanks on their part, but nobody, including the fisherman, remotely believed they were trying intentionally not to be thankful. Indeed, the remaining whales had lost many of their companions, and we would never know how many of the younger whales released that morning would survive to be adults. The older ones will probably have improved prospects. A little while later it looked like the two pods offshore had merged together, and we considered that to be a positive sign.

Understandably, the whales released from the beach were traumatized, firstly by the actual beaching, secondly by the confinement on the beach, thirdly by the unnatural mode of return to open water and fourthly, by the disorientation caused by the whole ordeal. All of this was atypical of life in their natural surroundings. It would take time for them to adjust to their marine habitat again, and more importantly, there's the psychological aspect of trying to locate immediate family members who might no longer be alive. Since the social development is so strong in this species, there were probably mothers seeking children and children longing for mothers. We know that the lactation period can exceed three years, so the mother-child bond is very important. For the larger males, the social importance may not be so crucial because they are known to leave one pod and go to another.

We all ask ourselves the question: Why do pilot whales run onto beaches? Was the lemming instinct also evident among some whale species, or did something more provocative have a part to play? Why do pilot whales in particular display this type of behaviour? We know that such behaviour is completely out of the ordinary and somewhat unorthodox and totally unexplained. However, the tendency to come ashore is displayed by the odontocetes group of whales in particular.

Most all beachings on the east coast of Canada have involved pilot whales, and there is no evidence to suggest any one particular cause. It appears to happen in areas with gently sloping coasts and beaches, and that was certainly the situation in this particular case. Whale strandings have also occurred around Sable and Cape Breton islands in Nova Scotia, the Gulf of St. Lawrence and the Bay of Fundy.

No earthquake could be blamed for this particular beaching. There's also no known sonar activities taking place or seismic operations to account for it. The close social development among pilot whales may have been a factor. Maybe one of the leading whales became disoriented for some reason and headed for the beach, with the remaining whales following. The fact that part of the original pod was still swimming around in the bay indicates that they must have detected the danger and aborted swimming into the shallower water.

CHAPTER FOUR

A SECOND BEACHING

Suddenly we become apprised of another situation that causes us more concern. About sixty metres from our site, twenty-eight whales beached themselves just as spontaneously and unpredictably as those in the first beaching. As a matter of fact, some of them had been on the beach before and released to safety. We know this because rope was still on their tails where it was severed during release. Exactly how many in this second beaching was part of the number we had previously released could not be determined. This same experience had been witnessed before in pilot whale rescue attempts in other locations. Unexplained and really unusual. It is thought that it might be a response to distress calls being emitted from whales on the beach.

Assuming the small pod of whales that was originally part of the main herd was socially intact, the whales that we released would likely bear kinship to most of those still on the beach. Therefore, when they were released there was probably no social response from those still present in the bay. The released whales would need to have comfort of some kind before deciding to join with them offshore. That would have to be from some kind of maternal outreach or a basic decision to simply join them, since they had no other alternative.

There's very little we can do for the whales involved in this second beaching. The tide is well down and the animals are not in good condition, as evidenced by their slow and infrequent movements. They were completely exhausted by the time we found them. Concentration by us in trying to save whales at the other end of the beach had permitted these whales to slip ashore unnoticed. The combination of hot sun, sand, and a falling tide ruined any chance for a return to the sea.

The relative assistance through human effort can now be measured. Nothing more could be accomplished to ensure continued life for the remaining creatures on the beach. Death would take its toll until the last whale succumbed. For some of them, this amounted to almost another twenty-four hours.

Many people are still pouring water over the whales to cool them as they lay on the beach, thereby easing their passing hours. Children are asking their parents, "How did they get here? Why did they swim up on the beach? Will they all die? Why didn't they swim off the beach again? If I keep putting water on them will they stay alive? How long will they stay alive?"

Everyone was just trying to make some sense of it all, but many questions did not have an answer. We can only use conjecture about the fate of these ocean creatures, who for some reason, interrupted their offshore migration leading to this catastrophe. It is an event that pods of long-finned pilot whales appear to share and answers are still being sought. You would expect that the close social development innate in these animals to be a more positive attribute rather than a reason for fatal accidents. Following the leader or leaders as part of the social activity of a whale pod may not be serving the whales well in cases like this. However, there is no doubt that it has positive advantages as well, such as obtaining food and propagation of the species.

Populations of long-finned pilot whales are estimated to be around 31,000 in the northwest Atlantic and another 750,000 in the central and eastern Atlantic, but in the latter area it could be as high as 1.4 million. Apart from strandings, incidental capture in fishing nets and natural fatalities, the populations appear to be sustainable and growing. The ban on the killing of all whales, with a few exceptions, has triggered a rebound in their populations. Killings now are mainly related to whale/boat collisions.

Adults and children are still walking the beach among the whales like walking through a hospital ward, stopping now and again to reach out and touch them. The size of the animals and the closeness to them amazed a lot of the younger set. Most had only read about whales in books or seen them on television, but now they were there among them, albeit not in their rightful marine habitat. They are bewildered by what they are seeing compared to what some of them had read about whales in the open seas. This might be the one and only time they will experience the whales up close.

Berkley and I surveyed the beach scene again and wondered aloud if we could have done more to get additional whales to safety. The odds were great because the circumstances surrounding the beaching gave little hope for too much success. But all involved tried anyway. Fishers and a few others who helped directly did yeomen service trying to beat the odds. Yet, as we look across the stretch of beach amid the dying whales and the people walking among them, we do not have a feeling of much accomplishment.

The monitoring of salmon rivers that we had planned for this day certainly was changed rather abruptly with Albert's phone call.

CHAPTER FIVE

WHALE RELEASE
TEAM ARRIVES

In the late afternoon, Dr. Jon Lien and his Memorial University whale research team arrive from St. John's. Once on the scene, they take over and carry out their research work by observing each animal and recording their last sounds. Dr. Keith Hay, a cetologist with Canada's Department of Fisheries and Oceans, also arrives, and along with a technician, begin research work immediately. Without knowing it, the mammals have donated their bodies to science and become martyrs in their own cause. Sometimes autopsies are necessary to add to our knowledge and allow science to move ahead to find ways and means for preventing similar occurrences.

Cetologists gather the evidence.
(Bill and Clara Tibbo)

As the onlookers gradually depart the area, Dr. Lien's team move from whale to whale, easing where possible inevitable death and recording their sometimes shrill and faint dying sounds. Would it be possible to decipher their meaning in a human context? Will we finally have the answer to this whale beaching phenomena? Only time will tell.

In addition to helping on the beach, Dr. Lien and his team are deeply concerned about the remaining pod still out in the bay. Would they decide to beach themselves? With this possibility in mind, a few team members took to rubber boats to analyze sea approaches to the bay and make a decision on the best escape route for the whales. One had to be careful at this point in time because any unusual action in the vicinity of the whales could provoke them toward detrimental action. After a cursory evaluation, it was decided to wait until dawn Sunday to entice the mourning survivors to freedom.

First light showed promise for a beautiful day. Dr. Lien has mustered his team, and preparations are made to try and herd the whales to a safe outlet. Rubber boats crewed by enthusiastic team members are launched quietly and quickly into the bay as the soft morning breeze and calm water display a delightful comparison to the previous day. Approaching the whales and positioning themselves properly, based on experience, the team abruptly moves in on the animals, trying to herd them as cowboys herd cattle. Some team members dropped salutes, very small explosives, in the water, and when the whales begin moving in the desired direction, there's no turning back. Amid tail-splashing and geyser-like water spouts, they swim to complete freedom in the open sea. For them at least, the temporary confinement was a successful detour on their planned migration route. Shouts go out from team members as the last pothead disappears through the channel and the natural safety of deeper water.

Questions remain in the minds of those responsible for directing them to the open sea. Will the young whales be fully accepted by other members of the pod? Will the survival rate of younger whales be lessened as a result of this mishap, or will they be fully protected by adult members of the pod? How will the death of the female whales of breeding age affect the overall pod? Will this pod be able to function satisfactorily on its own, or will it merge with another pod or herd? The answers will be played out in the ocean and we will have no way of knowing the outcome.

We knew that forty whales had been released from the original beaching. It was also known that twenty-eight were involved in the second beaching and at least some of those were of the same forty. The worst-case scenario would be that all twenty-eight were part of the forty whales initially released, although it appeared that some of them did mix with the pod lurking offshore. There is no way to know with certainty from our observation point. However, through the efforts of Dr. Lien and his crew, the successful escape of the whales remaining from the original pod was positive. Again, this number could not be determined exactly, but was estimated to be at least twenty-five. In all, the total effort related to the initial pod included saving at least twelve whales after the fact (after the beaching) plus herding twenty or more to safety and away from another potential beaching. Unfortunately, more of the pod remained dead than alive after the ordeal.

Throngs of visitors, estimated to be about one thousand, visited the site on Saturday, and at least double that number on Sunday. It being a weekend, many endeavoured to load the family in the car and motor to Point au Gaul to at least see the whales in close-up fashion. The curiosity of many had been aroused by the radio and television reports of the incident. Reporters were calling from many different locations in North America to obtain and report the news about the pilot whales. Local traffic became so intense on Sunday afternoon that the highway became blocked entirely, barring both entry and departure. The RCMP had to be summoned to get traffic moving again. Never before had local residents witnessed this number of people in their area. One town on the route set up a toll gate to raise money for the purchase of firefighting equipment, thereby capitalizing on this once-in-a-lifetime opportunity.

Obviously the plight of the whales piqued the interest of many people and not only locally. I suppose the sheer number of the beached whales had an effect on the apparent interest. The curiosity of many people faded after the initial attempt to free them was completed.

As the dead and dying animals lay on the beach, the visitors continued to pass by in mournful procession. Comments ranged from:

"How, when, and why did they come ashore?"

"Too bad they had to die!"

"I suppose it is all part of nature's plan! I guess it is God's will!"

"What a shameful waste of life!"

"Don't they look pitiful? Couldn't somebody have done something?"

"Why did so many come ashore?"

Then there was one little girl who put her arms around a metre-long dead whale and said, "Daddy, will this one come alive if I pour water over him?"

Her father replied apologetically, "I don't think so, but you can pour water over him anyway if you want," as she began heading toward the ocean with her bucket and her father's hand in tow.

It was uncanny to see children leaning against the large mammals that in their natural state would be swimming freely in the open ocean. It made the episode of the day a whole lot more unrealistic. Older children knew the gravity of the situation and were looking for answers while many younger ones looked in awe without full realization of the eventful tragedy. Very likely they may never witness such a scene again.

Reminds me of the story of a young boy and his dad walking along the beach when they happened upon a dead seagull. The boy looked at his dad and asked for an explanation. His father replied, "The gull died and went to Heaven."

The boy had another look at the gull and staring at his father, said, "I guess God didn't like him and threw him back."

How can you explain the massive number of whale fatalities and the scene before us on the beach? Unexplainable as it is, such are the phenomena that take place in nature.

CHAPTER SIX

DEALING WITH THE AFTERMATH

On Monday emphasis shifted from concern for whale life to the more morbid concern for carcass disposal. Avenues were sought to determine whether use could be made of the whale meat, but without result. Finally, the Provincial Department of Environment began arranging for the burial. Somehow or other, this part of the episode did not appear to fit with the quick pace and anxiety associated with the scene after the beaching. Instead of biologists dealing with life, we had pseudo-undertakers dealing with death. However, it was a task that had to be done.

The whales' gravesite on the beach.
(G. Snow)

A burial site was selected about one-half kilometre along the same beach where the whales had come ashore. Frank Corbett of Provincial Environment was in charge of the whale disposal operation. The sheer magnitude demanded a full-scale effort, and Frank obtained the services of three "Euclid" trucks, a front-end loader, and a bulldozer. The massive amount of mechanical and human energy required underlined the gigantism of this tragic event. It was Thursday before the cleanup was completed. As I watched the last whale disappear into the earthly tomb, thoughts of Saturday flashed through my mind and the initial struggle for life after the whales had propelled themselves ashore. There had to be some environmental or external interference that prompted the beaching. This is especially true in the case of the pregnant female whales, because in nature it doesn't appear logical for females to deliberately run aground and then as a final gesture give birth prematurely. Something was definitely out of balance.

**A truck used to haul the mammals to their final resting place.
(G. Snow)**

The community of Point au Gaul looked peaceful in the afternoon sun as the subdued peace and quiet returned. The beach appeared unscathed as the tidal action had obliterated any trace of the past few days. Residents are left only with the memories of those marine intruders who for some unknown reason had become trapped on the beach to die on their doorstep. They can be content in knowing that they, along with their neighbours from nearby Lamaline, did their utmost to free the marine creatures, and more are still alive because of their efforts and the work of Dr. Lien's team.

Dr. Jon Lien began his work with whales in 1979 as a result of the many reports of whales around the coast of Newfoundland that become entangled in commercial fishing nets. The intent was to make every effort to release the whales from nets with the dual purpose of saving the whales and also reduce the costs for fishers by reducing the damage to their nets. He initially had a team working with him that responded to calls from fishers when they encountered whales in their fishing gear. I had occasion to assist him and his team financially through my employment with Fisheries and Oceans in later years. Although Dr. Lien passed away in 2010 his legacy with the whales lives on. A protégé, Wayne Ledwell, heads up a non-profit group that responds to calls concerning accidental capture of whales in fishing nets and also includes turtles and sharks as well.

Many theories have been advanced to explain whale beachings. They include: parasitic infestation that could affect the whale's senses; oil pollution; sickness; action of large seagoing vessels; polluted coastal waters; heavy seas and strong currents; chasing prey such as squid; loud noises like seismic operations; calving; sonar echoes; and natural suicide. Scientists are still trying to find out the real cause, if there is one. All indications point to multiple causes.

In this particular beaching we had undulating seas striking a very gradual and sloping shoreline, a number of very young whales, but also larger adults and females close to calving. In navigating the rocky, rough, adjacent shoreline of Point au Gaul, the whales through parental instinct, may have sought more favourable sea conditions in the bay. They entered their sheltered area on the rising tide and before having the opportunity to adjust to the more confined surroundings, probably became panic stricken. As sometimes occurs during rising tide, the water often floods an area for a very short time but subdues quickly again. These whales may have been unlucky enough to be caught in such a sequence.

Whales are protected so it is conceivable that with increasing numbers there will continue to be encounters with nets around Newfoundland and Labrador. However, during the past twenty years there has been a lesser number of nets and traps used by fishers due to the declining groundfish stocks. Having witnessed the entanglement of humpback whales in fishing gear and the subsequent release by Dr. Lien and his team, be assured it is very gratifying from a conservation point of view and most often beneficial to fishers who own the nets. It is not an easy task to release whales from fishing gear, because you have to be in very close proximity to the animals when trying to cut the netting from their bodies to give them freedom. As long as whales are around, there will be accidental entanglements in fishing nets, but increased knowledge and effort will decrease such incidents and prevent whale fatalities.

A number of fishers have become more proficient at releasing whales from their own nets. Sometimes this is done by receiving instructions from the Whale Release Team who can provide them with information based on each specific entanglement. Mobile phones are helpful in this regard.

Albert Dodge and his fellow fishermen were left to ply their fishing trade. I'm sure every time a pothead whale was sighted on the fishing grounds, their minds returned to that particular July day. Perhaps the work of scientists like Dr. Lien, his successive team and cetologists, among others around the world, will eventually provide the answer to this strange animal behaviour. I hope it can be determined. At the moment it remains an unexplained mystery of marine life, and we can still only bear witness and contemplate the cause or causes. Regardless, we trust that pilot whales will continue to propagate, and the eventful intrusion like the one in Point au Gaul will become less common. They will continue to be a source of delight for observers and remain part of the Atlantic Ocean ecosystem.

Ecotourism has given many people an opportunity to see them in their natural marine surroundings, and major tourism operations have been developed in many parts of the world to facilitate it. The migration patterns of whales and the substantial distances involved mean that whales can be observed in different locations at different times of the year. For those of us who have witnessed whales this way, it is an awesome sight and a tremendous marine experience.

A bulldozer covers the last remains.
(G. Snow)

TAXONOMY OF PILOT WHALES

Phylum	Chordata
Class	Mammalia
Order	Cetacea
Family	Delphinidae
Genus	Globicephala
Species	Melaena

Pilot whales are in the same family (Delphinidae) as dolphins, but are considered the largest of the dolphin family, along with orcas. While pilot whales and orcas are in the same family, the orcas grow larger and are more diversified in their prey by consuming everything from herring to small whales, sharks, and seals.